Welcomed Wisdom

Book One of the
Wisdom for **L**iving **I**n **F**aith & **E**mpowerment
(L.I.F.E.) Series

Clytemnestra L. Clarke

Foreword by Co-Pastor Susie C. Owens

Welcomed Wisdom: Book One of the Wisdom for Living In Faith & Empowerment (L.I.F.E.) Series. Copyright ©2012 by Clytemnestra L. Clarke

Scripture references noted "AMP" are taken from the Holy Bible, Amplified Version. Copyright © 1954, 1958, 1962, 1964, 1965, 1987 by The Lockman Foundation. All rights reserved.

Scripture references noted "CEB" are taken from the Holy Bible, Common English Version. Copyright © 2011 by Common English Bible. All rights reserved.

Scripture references noted "ESV" are taken from the Holy Bible: English Standard Version. Copyright © 2001, Wheaton: Good News Publishers. Used by permission. All rights reserved.

Scripture references noted "KJV" are taken from the Holy Bible, King James Version. Public Domain.

Scripture references noted "NIRV" are taken from the Holy Bible, New International Reader's Version. Copyright © 1996, 1998 by Biblica, Inc.™ All rights reserved.

Scripture references noted "NIV" are taken from the Holy Bible, New International Version. Copyright © 1973, 1978, 1984 by International Bible Society. Used by permission of Zondervan Bible Publishers. All rights reserved.

Scripture references noted "NKJV" are taken from the Holy Bible, New King James Version. Copyright © 1982 by Thomas Nelson, Inc. Used by permission. All rights reserved.

Scripture references noted "NLT" are taken from the Holy Bible, New Living Translation. Copyright © 1996. Used by permission of Tyndale House Publishers, Inc., Wheaton, Illinois 60189. All rights reserved.

I'm Blest Indeed by Rosie Stogsdill

Cover design and author's photo: Go Pro Image
Senior Editor: Cynthia Norfleet Donaldson
Publishing Consultant: Obieray Rogers (www.rubiopublishing.com)

ISBN 978-1493773022

All rights reserved. No part of this publication may be reproduced, stored in a retrieval system, or transmitted in any form or by any means electronic, mechanical, photocopy, recording or otherwise except for brief extracts for the purpose of review, without the prior permission of the publisher and copyright owner.

Dedication

*Welcomed Wisdom is dedicated to the memory of three women
who touched my life in a powerful way.
Without their influence and example, I would not
be the woman I am today.*

Betty Gray Lawson
January 8, 1936 — December 27, 1998

Elizabeth Wise Copeland
August 31, 1923 — January 13, 2006

Viola Janie Cray
March 31, 1910 — August 18, 1988

Acknowledgments

I would like to thank and acknowledge each pastor's spouse who participated in *Welcomed Wisdom*—Mary Dargan, Doris Davis, Tina Dillard, Precious Earley, Mayme Flewellen, Matt Flowers, Joyce Foggs, Joyce Fowler, Sheryl Glover, Robin Green, Shirley McClure, Deborah McDowell, Tatum Osbourne, Felecia Pearson Smith, Ruby Perkins, Deborah Reeves, Karen Spencer, and Marilynn White. Your willingness to be open and transparent will no doubt be helpful and encouraging to countless pastors' spouses. Thank you for stretching along with me.

To Obie Rogers who patiently helped me to stay focused and motivated until I finally finished this project—even though I started it over 20 years ago!

To YoLanda Lewis for her help and encouragement with this project. Not only are we family, but we are friends. You have been and continue to be there for me. Love you!

To Marilynn White who is indeed a sister beloved. Thanks for all of your assistance. I couldn't have done this without you.

To my girlfriends and pastor's spouses (Priscilla Franklin, Felecia Pearson Smith, and Marva Scott) who are the sisters I never had. Thank you for being a friend. You all were there from the beginning and I will always be grateful for your love and support.

To the women I consider sisters and friends: Lady Patricia Ross, Dr. Roberta Turner, Minister Brenda Troy, First Lady Trina Jenkins, and First Lady Carolyn Miles. I've admired you over the years and appreciate the dignity and respect you have brought to the role of a pastor's spouse.

To Co-Pastor Susie Owens, thank you for your encouragement and support and for believing in me.

To Pastor Bridget Hilliard, thank you for showing me how to be a woman who wins!

To my beautiful daughters—Dionesha (Ocie), and Joscelyn; my grandson Ryan, my granddaughter London, my father Robert Lawson, and my brother Vincent (Angela) and his family—I love you all!

And, finally, to the special gift that God blessed me with 37 years ago—my husband, Bishop Timothy J. Clarke. Little did I know that God was up to something ginormous when he allowed our paths to cross. Thank you for selecting me to be your partner in life and love. It's been a wonderful journey. I love you dearly!

Foreword

First Lady Clytemnestra L. Clarke is a true and resonant example of one who ventures to share her experiences and wealth of wisdom gleaned from her life's journey. She has accomplished a masterful feat through the writing and collaborative authorship of *Welcomed Wisdom*.

I applaud Lady Clarke and I am delighted to acclaim, commend, and share what I've found to be a powerful and inspiring resource for pastors' wives throughout the body of Christ. This book is destined to enlighten, educate, and empower; at the same time, it will assuredly yield insight, inspiration, and impartation from some of the most experienced pastors' wives in the country. Be prepared to shift from the posture of feeling overwhelmed, frustrated, and hopeless to a privileged place of refreshing, renewal, and restoration!

Lady Clarke does a phenomenal job of ensuring that this writing is real, relatable, and relevant to the everyday challenges faced by many First Ladies. From the beginning and throughout, this book is riveted with pearls of wisdom and nuggets of spiritual weaponry, all designed to equip and prepare readers to rise above and properly handle the common and unique trials that knock at a First Lady's door.

Lady Clarke is most assuredly a woman fit for the Master's use as she willingly, and in such a transparent fashion, shares her own story. She leads out in the introduction with the stimulating candor that "if she only knew then what she knows now." That very thought undoubtedly led to the manifestation of this book, as it depicts her selfless character and her clarion call to aid, mentor, and coach others along their journey.

She is to be commended on her efforts to integrate a variety of resources, to ensure that a wealth and depth of valued servants were assembled to speak to varied backgrounds, seasons, and dynamics, while addressing the many issues represented throughout this book. In this profound sharing, Lady Clarke brings those who are fortunate to read this book to the realization that it's okay to be you; that God can see you through grief and illness; and it's okay to find a safe place to go for support. Through the contributors' outpouring, readers are admonished to seek a spiritual check-up, manage conflict, and maintain a posture of prayer. This book is an invigorating and insightful truth!

While she dares to keep it real and leave no stone uncovered in this page turner, Lady Clarke and others skillfully polish off each chapter with attainable steps that will leave you leaping over obstacles, barriers, and walls that can seem unbearable. You will be encouraged to meditate, reflect, and engage in the steps necessary to believe God on a renewed spiritual level.

Lady Clarke transcends all potential limits and delivers a mechanism that demonstrates a most valuable teaching, motivating readers to continue their God-given destiny as a First Lady. What an honor and privilege to be chosen to walk beside a man of God—to be his helpmeet—and to aid in nurturing the people he is called to serve.

With great resolve, Lady Clarke carefully sets out to categorically relay truth specifically for First Ladies who desire to walk out their roles and to stroll through this journey with all the joy, peace, harmony, fulfillment, and vigor that God desires for us to have; this is attainable.

Throughout the pages of *Welcomed Wisdom*, Lady Clarke and others send a resounding message that will arm you with graceful solutions for potentially grave situations.

Lady Clarke has shared invaluable wisdom that I've deemed as a useful tool and practical guidance. This book is undeniably written to help First Ladies soar to heights unimaginable, as God mandates it in this time, season, era, and beyond.

Prepare to be propelled!

Most Gracious Regards,

Evangelist Susie C. Owens, D. Min.
Co-Pastor, Greater Mt. Calvary Holy Church, Washington, DC
International First Lady, Mt. Calvary Holy Church of America, Inc.

Table of Contents

Introduction: Wisdom's Journey 1

"If I Only Knew Then What I Know Now" 3

Chapter One: Wisdom Secures 9
"Uniquely Me" 11
"Finding My Ministry Voice" E. Joyce Fowler 13
"Do You" Felecia Pearson Smith 17
"A Pastor's Wife: Before and After" Shirley McClure 19

Chapter Two: Wisdom Comforts 23
"Good Grief" 25
"No One Is Exempt" Deborah M. Reeves 29

Chapter Three: Wisdom Supports 33
"Family Matters" 35
"God Speaks to Me Plain" Robin H. Green 39
"A New Perspective" Marilynn White 41

Chapter Four: Wisdom Heals 43
"In Sickness and In Health" 45
"The Blessing of Hearing and Believing God Is at Work" Mary L. Dargan 47
"Healing Through Prayer Walking" Ruby A. Perkins 49

Chapter Five: Wisdom Teaches 51
"Spiritual Check-Up" 53
"What's Impeding Your Progress?" Tatum M. Osbourne 55
"How Did I End Up Here?" Precious A. Earley 57

Chapter Six: Wisdom Learns 61
"Managing Conflict" 63
"Changed" Sheryl D. Glover 65

Chapter Seven: Wisdom Directs 67
"Where Do I Go? Who Do I Go To?" 69
"God's Got It" Deborah McDowell 71
"Find Your Place in God" Doris K. Davis 75

Chapter Eight: Wisdom Leads 77
"Women's Ministry: Mind, Body, and Spirit" 79
"Growing Into a First Lady" Tina T. Dillard 81
"Don't Miss the Treasure" Karen R. Spencer 83

Chapter Nine: Wisdom Intercedes 87
"Prayer Works" 89
"The Joy and Rewards of Obedience" Mayme Flewellen 91

Chapter Ten: Wisdom Speaks 95
"I Do" 97
"How Strong Is Your Marriage?" Joyce D. Foggs 99

Chapter Eleven: Wisdom Loves Beyond Limits 105
"Leading From Behind" 107
"A Male Perspective" Matt Flowers 109

Conclusion: Wisdom Honors 111
"Growing, Growing, Grown" 113

Contributors 115

Introduction
Wisdom's Journey

"We can make our plans, but the Lord determines our steps."
(Proverbs 16:9, NLT)

"If I Only Knew Then What I Know Now"

There was no doubt in my mind that after completing my educational endeavors, pursuing my career goals, and exploring the world, I would one day settle down and enjoy married life with the man of my dreams. Having seen a first-hand example of the marital commitment my parents experienced, I grew up understanding the concept that marriage was "till death do us part." In my mind, that sounded like forever, so it was important to me that I not miss what God had for me, while looking for what I thought I wanted or needed.

After several feeble attempts at dating, I finally decided that it was time for me to factor myself out of the equation and to allow God to work on my behalf. It was obvious that my method wasn't working, but I never imagined that God would work in such a mysterious way. I never imagined that God would take me down a path that only He had the directions for. Never could I imagine that He would deem me worthy of what I consider a special honor and privilege.

Over 38 years ago, I received a special invitation into the world of a wonderful man with a great personality, big heart, and winning ways. He just seemed to be ideal husband material. He was very articulate and intelligent, and had a commanding presence. He had a deep sultry voice and was over six feet tall. He had a biggie-sized heart and, more importantly, he loved the Lord and he loved me!

My mother (bless her memory) jumped into the situation with both feet and was my intercessor (or should I say, interceptor?). I translated her intervention tactics as her saying, "Girl, don't be stupid! This is a good one. You better not let him get away!" On the other hand, my father was a little suspect of this new love interest. He was giving side eyes every opportunity he had. But even with the excitement and thrill of it all, I had only one concern—he was a preacher! As a matter of fact, he was one of the best I had ever heard. At that point in my life I can't say that I was an authority on spiritual matters, but I had just enough discernment to know that there was something different, special, and unique about this man that made me believe and know that God definitely had His hand on his life.

I guess there's a lot to be said about young love. When you have youth, strength, vim, vigor, and vitality on your side, mixed with some love, you feel like you can conquer anything, including the world! Remember that concern I said I had? Well, it began to dissipate as I began to believe that this was the man and this was the course that God had charted for my life. On April 2, 1977, we sealed the deal and our journey began. I don't know if I could have been any greener than I was, but with God and now a new partner, I was ready for the adventure of my life.

It began with the call to pastoral leadership in 1978. My husband graciously accepted the call to pastor the York Avenue Church of God in Warren, Ohio. It was his first assignment as a pastor and my first attempt at being a pastor's spouse. To be totally honest, I had no clue as to what the congregation expected of me. Now, you have to remember this was a different kind of day. The word "co-pastor" hadn't made its way onto the scene and pastors' spouses weren't paid staff yet; so it occurred to me that I better go with what I know and just do the "traditional stuff" like singing in the choir, working with the children in Sunday School and VBS, and visiting the sick and shut-ins. Of course, there was a Baptist Ministers' Wives and Widows Organization. Interestingly enough, they held to the traditional roles of a pastor's spouse and it was cute to see them all sitting together at community-wide services wearing their hats and gloves. I didn't even own a hat or a pair of gloves, so that made me an instant reject. By all indications, I didn't even qualify to walk—let alone run—in that circle. Besides, I normally ended up sitting in the back with my active two-year-old, who I had to carry out at least two or three times before the end of service.

Looking back on those years in Warren, I can truly say that it was an experience that prepared me for the next move of God in our lives. I met many wonderful people and forged some friendships that are still a vital part of my life today. Warren helped me mature spiritually. I learned valuable lessons that I could never have otherwise learned apart from going through not only the pleasant, but also the difficult and challenging experiences. When my husband and I moved to Warren, we had only been married about a year; and then later on in our first year there, we had our first child. What a blessing! However, we didn't have any family to help us and it was hard to know whom to trust, which only made us depend on each other and God all the more.

As our family grew, our Church family grew as well. It was great to see the Church thriving and souls being won to the Kingdom. We had finally settled in and felt that since God had placed us there, then we were going to serve to the best of our ability. Now in my heart, I was praying that God had not forgotten about us. I trusted my husband enough to believe that if God had told him to remain in Warren for the duration of his time in ministry, then he and I both were going to have major crowns and mansions awaiting us when we reached the other shore! But in my spirit, I always believed that God sent us there for a season of preparation for the next leg of our journey, and I will always be grateful for that. That preparation was invaluable as we transitioned to the next phase of ministry. Just when the Church was at its peak, the Lord released us from York Avenue and directed us to First Church of God in Columbus, Ohio. The congregation called us to the work in Columbus in November 1981, and we moved there in February 1982. It was also the year that our family expanded once again and our second child was born.

Even though we came to a small congregation of less than 100 members, they were a loving, giving people who immediately won my heart. By now I was a semi-pro at this pastor's spouse thing. After all, this was round two and this time I had a little experience under my belt.

I remember arriving in Columbus with the same question looming in the back of my mind: What expectations would this new congregation have of me? The only difference this time was I was not pressed and I understood that there wasn't a need to impress. I knew that I needed to be still long enough for the Lord to direct me to the areas in which He would have me to serve, and He did.

It was amazing to watch the congregation grow. As preaching went forth, the congregation expanded and filled up to capacity. As the congregation continued to grow, it became obvious that there was a need to build, so we went through building phase number one. It was refreshing to see the congregation, which had now expanded to over 500, follow leadership and rally as we entered into a building campaign. It wasn't long before the campaign was completed and we moved into our new structure.

I remember the first Sunday we moved into our new sanctuary. As a choir member, I was sitting in the choir stand surveying the audience. I saw a number of half full pews and an empty balcony, and I wondered to myself if the new structure would fill up as quickly as the old one had; thank God, it did!

The interesting thing is that this scenario would occur again several years later as the Lord continued to add to the Church. It was then that we were blessed to acquire 124 acres of land where the "City of Refuge" is now located with over 6,000 members. That's sure a long way from the less than 100 members we found when we first came to Columbus.

It has been a humbling experience to see God work and move in such powerful ways over the years. Even more humbling is the fact that He trusted us with such a mammoth undertaking. From the time we arrived in Columbus until now, everything that I have experienced—good, bad, or indifferent—has enriched my life and helped me to develop into the First Lady I am today. But, let's not get things twisted. Throughout my years in ministry, things have not always been perfect or without struggle. But regardless of where I find myself, the stabilizing force for me is my belief that God has charted the course of my life according to Psalm 139. I know I can trust God to navigate all of the circumstances of my life and that His faithfulness is great.

Throughout the rest of this book I will share the wisdom and experiences I've had up to this point in my life. If I had known from the beginning what I know now, I would have had a stellar journey. I've come to learn that the way you can be a blessing to others is to go through life's challenges and detours. This qualifies you for the position. As pastors' spouses, we are called on to touch the lives of those we come in contact with or anyone God places in our paths. What better way to do so than from the vantage point of empathy and compassion?

I am excited because not only will I be sharing my experiences, but you will also be able to benefit from the experiences of 18 other pastors' spouses from across the country. Like me, they signed up for the adventure of their lives. I believe you'll find their stories rich in thought, content, and details as they share wisdom from the wells of their experiences:

- Some are new to ministry and come with a fresh perspective as the role of pastors' spouses has shifted, elevated, and evolved over the years.

- Others will recount their experiences from years of wisdom that have allowed them to evolve into their individual roles in ministry, while still serving in a more traditional role.

- Yet others will speak from a voice and position of authority and experience as they now define their role in ministry from a new season of their lives that includes transitioning from an active ministry role to that of a mentor or coach, which is a nice way of saying they've retired!

So you see, it will be exciting to read the compilation of years of ministry experiences shared by seasoned and contemporary voices. While designed for pastors' spouses, *Welcomed Wisdom* also has the unique ability to minister, impact, and speak to the heart of a person whose spouse serves or works in any leadership capacity. There are basic concepts that are applicable to any leadership role. You will find this book to be an easy read that you can understand, appreciate, and relate to. You will also find many similarities and parallels to your own life story. Keep reading; I'm sure there's something that will definitely bless and benefit you.

Chapter One
Wisdom Secures

"I will praise thee; for I am fearfully and wonderfully made: marvellous are thy works; and that my soul knoweth right well."
(Psalm 139:14, KJV)

"Uniquely Me"

As a pastor's spouse, I have found that many women within the congregation look to us as their role model, example, or spiritual mentor. What I have found over the years is that there are many women within our congregations who may not have been "churched" or had the advantage or benefit of being mothered or mentored. So they cast a watchful eye on you and they take their cues from your actions and reactions, even down to your hairstyle, what you wear, or your mannerisms. You would really be surprised just how much you're being watched.

There is always the temptation to perform in your role as the pastor's spouse. You know. . .the smiling and nodding; always being full of encouragement and kind words; always being the main cheerleader for your husband—whether he's hitting a home run that Sunday or not. I mean, after all, the congregation is watching and, therefore, you must be on your best behavior.

That all sounds okay if you've perfected the role and have been at it for awhile. But what if you're new at it? How do you maintain the genuine and authentic you without losing yourself to a scripted role? Now, if the truth be known, a scripted role may help you if you know your personality is one that could be misunderstood; but for the most part, I believe you can have the best of both worlds. A blend of your personality and who you are, along with the responsibility of the role, are the perfect combination for a comfortable fit.

You see, if we're not careful, we will look to others to define our role. And while there's nothing wrong with gleaning wisdom and knowledge from others who have been godly examples, we must never become them or something other than who we are.

It didn't take me long to realize that I was wasting my time trying to be like some of the pastors' spouses that I so admired. It was exhausting and frustrating. It even made me feel that obviously I wasn't cut out for the assignment. But when I decided that it might be best for me to just "do me," I experienced freedom and release. When I realized that God had gifted me with everything I needed to get the job done, I ceased striving to be an imitation of someone else. Over the years I've looked at and turned to other pastors' spouses for wisdom and guidance, but I learned to remain loyal to the individual God made me to be. I believe our congregation appreciates me for that.

Being someone other than yourself puts an unnecessary pressure and burden on you and it minimizes your uniqueness. Even if you feel that who you are and what you have to offer may not be as great as what someone else has to offer, just know that someone needs what you have. God has uniquely gifted you for your assignment. Here's what I know. What works for me and my situation may not work for you and yours. Find your niche and serve to the glory of God. And, for heaven's sake, just "do you!"

It's important to understand that God has a purpose and plan for each of our lives. Our contributors have shared from an open and honest place; and as you read their stories, you will:

1. Begin to celebrate the importance of being comfortable with whom you are.

2. Appreciate the fact that there is a special place for your giftedness.

3. Agree with what God's Word says about you and praise God that you are fearfully and wonderfully made.

Continue reading and discover how these ladies arrived at their destination of uniqueness.

"Finding My Ministry Voice"
E. Joyce Fowler

I had the great privilege of being mentored by a mother whose chief desire was to be a minister's wife. She loved the Lord. Ministry was a primary desire of hers and she raised her children to respect ministers and the ministry.

I have always wanted to serve the Lord, but ministry...well, that was another story. I had no desire to marry a minister. In fact, it was one question I posed after my husband, a minister's son, proposed. "Do you think you will follow your father into full-time ministry?" I asked. He said emphatically, "No!" and I responded with equal enthusiasm, "Good!" I did not want to be a pastor's wife and I didn't need time to reflect on that issue. Living in the "bubble" was not anything I saw myself doing. Looking back on that experience, I can only say now in light of 42 years of serving as a First Lady, God must surely have a sense of humor!

I now stand in awe of God's grace and power. He turned two reluctant individuals into deeply committed servant leaders. For my husband, that meant ministry as an associate and later as a senior pastor. For me, it meant a ministry in caring for the wounded and afflicted, and supporting my companion in whatever ways possible.

Initially, I was very comfortable fulfilling the role of assisting my husband by greeting the saints, sitting close to the pulpit, and offering silent signals of support as my companion labored in the Word. Finding my ministry voice took time. Since serving as First Lady was not on my radar screen, I initially found it uncomfortable, even hard, to feel relaxed in the traditional role of a minister's wife. Because I needed to work full time as a registered nurse during our early years in the ministry, I often struggled with expectations. I was managing, but competing, with conflicting roles and demands as wife, mother, and Church leader. This conflict often caused me to retreat from some leadership roles in the Church. After all, you can only be stretched so far. Needless to say, I felt obligated due to exhaustion to reduce my availability for some leadership opportunities.

I followed a First Lady who was the complete opposite of me. She was not employed outside of the home and she was involved in many activities. She organized auxiliaries. She led community initiatives. She was very inspirational and encouraging. She possessed an inner authority that enabled her to seemingly draw people into whatever she was supporting. She was a great First Lady, and I admired her. Yet, my circumstances were different. I was fully aware of my gifts. I did not always follow the traditional expectations of being a pastor's wife.

It has often been said that time heals all wounds. There is an inner healing that comes with time. I am grateful that I persisted in the pursuit of my voice. Underscore the word "my." In time, I noticed people were not only drawn to me because of my genuine desire to affirm them through gestures and words, but also because I was able to help them, through my medical knowledge, to understand the human body.

Being a registered nurse, I was constantly asked by parishioners to explain the effects of the medications they were taking. (Strange as it may sound, I always enjoyed reading pharmaceutical catalogs). While I could answer most questions, I was always quick to advise them to talk with their physician and ask God for healing.

These conversations always occurred at Church. With the encouragement of my husband, I organized a medical board and began to offer information and screening services. And that is when it happened. I found my voice! This was my calling: Assisting others in their physical, emotional, and spiritual struggles to gain the information needed to sustain a healthy lifestyle. I always felt I was in the place God wanted me to occupy when I was serving others as a provider of information and health-related services. Physicians often expressed gratitude for my assistance to their patients. Church members allowed me to journey with them in their pursuit of peace of mind. Even when I had to gently scold the saints for failing to follow the medical advice they had been given, I had a feeling of contributing real value to their lives.

A sense of "arrival" came over me. I knew I was doing important work. I became increasingly convinced that this work was indeed God's work with each conference I helped organize; as each board member became energized through his or her involvement in the ministry of healing; and as each person we helped learned to manage their weaknesses and follow sound medical advice. We were exactly where God wanted us to be.

Our medical board arranged a men-only symposium on prostate cancer, lead by two top physicians in that field. I left that conference convinced that my work in preparing and hosting medical forums was directly linked to the Gospel of Jesus and the goal of the Church: Complete healing of body, mind, and spirit! I coined a phrase that became quite popular in and around the Church. I called it "Uniting the Healing Forces: Medicinal, Moderated, and the Miraculous." I wanted people to know that God cares for the whole person; that healing occurs on multiple levels; and that God wants us to go beyond physical healing to wellness of the soul, body, spirit, and relationships.

I can truly say I am blessed. More importantly, in finding my voice, I also found a stream of joy flowing throughout the services I lead. That is what I pray can happen to all who are privileged to occupy the position of a pastor's spouse.

I pray that you will find your ministry voice, as I have found mine. When you discover it and are faithful to it, get ready for God to open your eyes to the wonders of His love, as He uses you to guide people to better choices and wiser decisions.

There is no better choice we can make than to trust Jesus for our place of service within the Church. And there is no wiser decision we can make than to embrace the gifts and calling of God. I did, and in the process I made a great discovery—my ministry voice!

"Do You"
Felecia Pearson Smith

I have a very good friend who uses this phrase with me all the time: "Do you." She is known as Sister C. The first time she told me to "do you," I was whining about not being like other pastors' wives. I am loud and sometimes my personality does not make me feel as "spiritual" as some of my other First Lady friends. Whenever I am in one of these moods, Sister C says, "Girl, just do you!"

I have learned to embrace myself more these days than in earlier times. There was a period in my life when I even questioned why I was so vocal and opinionated, filtering life through a different lens. I had begun to feel that while I was a pastor's wife, I had been wired by God just a little bit differently. Whenever I would try to be someone other than who God had created me to be, I would feel a gentle nudge in my spirit in a way that only a friend can nudge you, saying, "Felecia, just do you."

What does it mean to "do you" in a world where pastors' wives, who live in such a public space, are tempted to emulate what others are doing? I was getting tired of trying to fit into a mold. In order to take my sister up on her challenge to "do you," I needed to know who "me" was. I could not "do" someone I did not know. Who was my true self, and what was my authentic voice? This inner journey would not be easy, but I felt Sister C's presence nudging me on.

The first thing I realized about myself was that I could not "do me" because I was "doing" everybody else. I was trying to fix my husband, my children, the Church, and everyone around me. I took pride in walking into a room and taking care of everyone and every project, yet neglecting the one person who needed help the most—me.

Over the years I had neglected self-care, which for many years was reflected in my constant dieting and trying to lose weight. Finally one day I decided to take care of myself. For me, this meant acknowledging my feelings and emotions, which I had buried and masked under all of the laughter. Don't get me wrong, I believe that my humor is one of the things that God has blessed me with; but it must not be used to cover pain, feelings, or emotions.

I also realized that I could not "do me" because I had allowed the busyness of life and ministry to become a substitute for solitude and silence in my life. Solitude was taking care of the outer distractions of my life, and silence was taking care of the inner distractions in my life. For me, this meant sitting, reflecting, and hearing from God. It meant that I was not doing all of the talking, but I was engaging in an authentic conversation with God and myself. My inability to do this had robbed me of authenticity in my relationship with God and with others. I needed to reclaim this spiritual discipline in my life. I wanted it badly. For me to "do," I would have to learn to "be."

Also, my trying to fix everyone and my busyness had robbed me of knowing what I desired or needed for my life. In her book *Sacred Rhythms,* Ruth Barton talks about blind Bartimaeus sitting by the road. When Jesus came by, Bartimaeus called out for Him. His cry actually aggravated the people and they wanted him to be quiet. Jesus raised the question, "What do you want me to do for you?" and Bartimaeus said, "I want to see." It was his desire to see.

Once I stopped trying to fix everyone and began to practice sitting, reflecting, and listening to God, I was able to articulate my true desires before God. I wanted to see: To see the real me, to see what it would be like to have an authentic relationship with God and others, to see the importance of always being real with God, and to see and to state my true needs and desires.

So today when I find myself drifting back into some of my old ways of trying to fix others and getting caught up in the busyness of life and ministry, I can hear my sister friend saying to me, "Felecia, do you." When her gentle voice resonates in my spirit, I find myself getting back to myself and "doing me."

"A Pastor's Wife: Before and After"
Shirley McClure

My story is much the same as other Church girls, although most of us don't choose to be transparent. I couldn't wait to get out of my parent's house and you know why—because of all those rules: Only Sunday-go-to-meeting clothes, no pants, no boyfriend, no secular music (except for Lawrence Welk), no going to the movies, no weekday TV, no junk food, and no clowning around. You better not get caught lying or stealing for that meant you were threatened with instant death, although talking back to an adult could get you killed first!

I did things but not because I disliked Church. To be honest, I did not know people disliked Church. In fact, after I got saved as a teenager, I usually had to get saved every Sunday because when you sinned, you had to repent openly and get saved all over again as a backslider. I had to do it, and sometime wondered why the older saints did not. I referred to them as hypocrites. I came to the conclusion, you don't play with God. Either you are in, or you are out. As a young adult, I got out. I was having fun but was never at peace with myself.

Yes, I got kicked out of high school for disrespecting a teacher and had to finish later. Yes, I suffered a crippling illness, only to be healed. Yes, I ran away from home to be with a man who was wanted for murder (unbeknownst to me). Yes, I eloped to get married. Yes, I had countless affairs while married to a nice husband. Yes, I got addicted to prescription drugs. And yes, I got in trouble with the law. I also tried to commit suicide and subjected myself to physical abuse, including a murder attempt on my life. All of this had happened to me by the age of 34, including a failed marriage and five children by three different men, while still married.

Yet, in my quiet time, I realized I was lost, unfulfilled, and hated what I had become. I was raised better than this by two good Christian parents who exemplified how a Christian should live. Whether I was just curious, stupid, or sheltered is hard to determine. I had the audacity to want a successful marriage and to live a Christian life as my parents did. Even in my wilderness, I still raised my children with love, strict rules, respect for others, and God. I didn't forget to threaten them with instant death for lying and stealing, at least that's what I wanted them to think. My motto was, "I brought you in this world, and I will take you out."

God knew about my struggle, for I had many discussions with Him about the matter. I wanted God, but not without a man. Well, I got both. Always knowing what I wanted, I had a vision of the man I wanted; I knew I wanted us to serve God together. I don't know if God felt my desire or had a plan for my life, but I got married again after a very short courtship. I married him on a Friday, and we rededicated our lives back to God that following Sunday, some 37 years ago.

I wish I could write "The End" and tell you we lived happily ever after, but that's not the case. My past came back to haunt my second marriage and reared its ugly head. What goes around comes around. God had tried to get my attention regarding my soul's salvation when two of my infant children suffered death through mishaps during my previous marriage. In those tragedies, I took comfort in that they were in heaven. But once again, I was forced to face the reality of what was becoming a struggling marriage, I had to decide whether or not I wanted the husband God gave me, or God alone. I decided without a doubt, God. Because He loves me, He completely restored me by allowing me to continue to have both.

I've fallen in love with this Salvation and the Church and they have become my lifestyle. After four years of working out the salvation of our souls, my husband, Rev. Dr. Robert McClure, Jr., was called to ministry. We learned how to forgive each other and ourselves, and how to live this Christian life; even going through Church conflicts added to our maturity as Christians. Like me, my husband fell in love with the work of the Church. We got involved in youth ministry at our affiliated churches, and even served in management on a national level after retirement from secular employment. As we showed ourselves approved by God and man, He gave us another assignment to pastor a Church—now for over 15 years.

Why me? I look back over my life and realize that my sordid past helps me to relate to the lost and struggling souls I come in contact with. During these last 15 years, I've taught at the local colleges, new members' classes, and Bible studies at my local Church; and I've conducted workshops upon request. Because of learned wisdom from God, I now have spiritual revelation:

- If you raise your children in the way they should go, they will return. I DID!
    - Train up a child in the way he should go, And when he is old he will not depart from it. (Proverbs 22:6, NKJV)

- You can be an overcomer by being transparent in relating to others in an effort to renew their minds. I DID!
    - And so, dear brothers and sisters, I plead with you to give your bodies to God because of all he has done for you. Let them be a living and holy sacrifice—the kind he will find acceptable. This is truly the way to worship him. Don't copy the behavior and customs of this world, but let God transform you into a new person by changing the way you think. Then you will learn to know God's will for you, which is good and pleasing and perfect. (Romans 12:1-2, NLT)

- Live pleasing to God and you will also be beneficial to man. I DID!
    - For the kingdom of God is not a matter of eating and drinking, but of righteousness, peace and joy in the Holy Spirit, because anyone who serves Christ in this way is pleasing to God and receives human approval. (Romans 14:17-18, NIV)

- While working physically close with your mate in the ministry, have your own ministry (get a life). I DID!
    - But you be watchful in all things, endure afflictions, do the work of an evangelist, fulfill your ministry. (2 Timothy 4:5, NKJV)

- Find support with other spiritual leaders to be encouraged or to encourage. I DID!
    - From Miletus he sent to Ephesus for the leaders of the congregation. When they arrived, he said, "You know that from day one of my arrival in Asia I was with you totally—laying my life on the line, serving the Master no matter what, putting up with no end of scheming by Jews who wanted to do me in. I didn't skimp or trim in any way. Every truth and encouragement that could have made a difference to you, you got. I taught you out in public and I taught you in your homes, urging Jews and Greeks alike to a radical life-change before God and an equally radical trust in our Master Jesus." (Acts 20:19-21, MSG)

- Walk humbly, be approachable, and remember to serve others. I DO!
    - But it shall not be so among you: but whosoever will be great among you, let him be your minister; And whosoever will be chief among you, let him be your servant; (Matthew 20:26-27, KJV)

Because my husband and I were older when we accepted the pastoral assignment and had already served on a national level, our exposure benefited our interaction with our members. My doctrinal background, management skills, God's wisdom, and even my past have allowed me to play an intricate part in others' lives and have contributed to my success as a First Lady. I personally ask to be respected but there's no need to cater to me. I'm just Sister Shirley!

Chapter Two
Wisdom Comforts

"When my father and my mother forsake me, then the Lord will take me up."
(Psalm 27:10, NKJV)

"Good Grief"

Anyone who has experienced a loss while in the midst of ministry will understand my heart as I recount this painful encounter.

I remember one conversation in particular as if it were yesterday. I was sitting in my office at work when I received a phone call from my mother telling me that she had received a report from the doctor saying that she had breast cancer. I can't even begin to express my emotional state after receiving the news except to say I was in a state of shock. All I could think of was what this might mean. How selfish of me. Here my mother had just shared what was probably the most devastating news of her life with me and all I could think of was how it was going to affect me. Once I gathered myself and my thoughts, I tried my best to assure my mother that I would do whatever was needed to help her get through the upcoming ordeal.

As time progressed, I found myself juggling family, work, school, Church, and caregiver responsibilities. Many days I sat at work with a divided heart and mind. Many days I struggled to stay focused on school assignments; it is nothing short of a miracle that I was able to finish on schedule. Many days I sat at Church with my heart there but my mind a thousand miles away. Many times at home I would find myself on autopilot as I handled the responsibilities of being a wife and mother.

My mother understood the scope and range of everything that I was doing and always reminded me that she didn't want to be a burden. In my mind she was never a burden, and it was my joy to minister to her during this critical period of her life. However, nothing stopped; life kept moving in the midst of my anticipatory grief and I felt like my world was spinning out of control.

About five years after that call, my mother passed away. I was left to find a way to manage my grief while trying to return to a routine lifestyle—a "new normal"—while maintaining a sense of composure by managing my emotions. Of course, I felt I had to be there for my dad, my brother, my kids, and all of the other family members. It never dawned on me that I needed to grieve, that I needed help, or that I needed comfort myself.

The truth is, my life would never be the same and my new reality was foreign and scary; I really didn't like it. There were many Sundays that I preferred not to attend services and I really didn't want to hear people asking me if I was all right, because I wasn't.

As I continued to work through my grief and the healing process, I discovered that I had to take my own medicine. You see, a portion of my unique position with the State of Ohio Employee Assistance Program afforded me the opportunity to provide service, help, and resources to state employees who have suffered the loss of co-workers and managers. After all, when you work with someone for eight plus hours a day, they become your work family whether you like them or not. My job allowed me to walk and talk co-workers through the stages of grief and to help them process and reach closure following the loss, so that they could return to productivity. There were times when I could sense the presence of the Lord with me, as I ministered to the employees without crossing boundaries.

I discovered that the same help and resources I would share with the employees applied to me as well, and that I wasn't exempted from the process. It was through my pain that I realized that God is a God of all comfort.

Through this experience I was better able to not only sympathize, but also empathize, with those who have experienced the loss of a significant loved one. I now share from my pain and experience; and the words I use are not just some generic phrases, but heartfelt and sincere.

Here are some final thoughts:

- The grieving process, while not comfortable, is necessary. There is emotional value in taking the time to process through your loss.

- Most of the time we view loss in a one-dimensional manner, but you can experience loss in ways other than death. There is the loss of relationships and friendships, the loss of confidence and courage, the loss of dreams and directions, and the list can go on and on. When these types of losses occur, you have to allow yourself the space to grieve and process through them as well.

- Don't go it alone. Allow other trusted individuals to minister to you. After all, you are there for others when they are in need. Understand that this is your time of need and then be open to receiving the help and support.

While death can take a loved one from us physically, it can *never* rob us of our memories. When you find yourself overwhelmed by grief, reflect on the happy moments shared with your loved one; it has a way of warming your heart and bringing a smile to your face. From time to time, you will experience moments of sadness, but good memories can be an antidote to grief and can help lift you out of the doldrums.

If you find that you are still experiencing sadness or even depression after a significant amount of time (I'm going to go out on a limb to say this, but oh well!), it may be necessary to seek professional help. Don't be ashamed to do so.

Even though your life may be different after the loss of a loved one, and you may feel lonely or abandoned, we do know that God is a God of all comfort. His Word tells us in Hebrews 13:5 (AMP) that "I will not, I will not, I will not to any level or degree, leave you helpless or without support." That, my sister, can be comfort enough.

> Precious memories, how they linger,
> How they ever flood my soul.
> In the stillness, of the midnight,
> Precious sacred scenes unfold.
> (*Precious Memories,* J. B. F. Wright, 1925)

I have walked through the grieving experience, and so has our next contributor. She shares practical wisdom and healing Scriptures that will help you work through the grieving process. Nothing brings peace and comfort like the Word of God as we deal with the tragedies of life. Allow what she has to say to minister to you.

"No One Is Exempt"
Deborah M. Reeves

Tragedy can strike any one at any time. I think most people can agree that surviving a tragedy is easy compared to surviving the aftermath of the tragedy. And, if you have not had a tragedy in your life, just keep on living.

Tragedies come in many forms, such as weather disasters, wars, loss of a limb, broken relationships, divorce, miscarriage, domestic violence, incarceration, death, job loss, medical issues, and so forth. People usually grieve because they have lost something that they love; or they are deprived of a loved one through death or miles of separation. The sense of loss is profound.

It is natural to feel anger, sadness, regret, fear, or anguish when going through a tragedy. But no matter what sort of difficulties or how painful the experience, the real tragedy happens when we lose hope. One mistake people often make during a tragedy is to shut other people out. Pulling away and keeping to oneself is not good. Don't shut God's people out. A very important part of the healing process is to keep godly family members, Church family, and friends close to you so that they can provide comfort and encouragement.

Many will ask, "How do I recover from such a tragedy?" Well, we already know the answer is not going to be cut and dry by any means. The recovery from any kind of tragedy doesn't feel good at all. Quite frankly, it hurts deeply. It takes time. It takes patience. It takes forgiveness. And, it takes love.

Healing is a process that God walks His people through moment to moment, day to day. This is not the time to give up or give in. I believe there are four steps to healing:

1. Get to know God.
2. Develop a genuine prayer life.
3. Share your pain and sorrow with God and expect deliverance.
4. Walk in your healing.

To enhance the four healing processes, please read and study the following Scriptures taken from the New King James Version:

Romans 8:28
> And we know that all things work together for good to those who love God, to those who are the called according to His purpose.

1 John 5:14-15
> Now this is the confidence that we have in Him, that if we ask anything according to His will, He hears us. And if we know that He hears us, whatever we ask, we know that we have the petitions that we have asked of Him.

Psalm 139:13-16
> For You formed my inward parts; You covered me in my mother's womb. I will praise You, for I am fearfully and wonderfully made; Marvelous are Your works, and that my soul knows very well. My frame was not hidden from You. When I was made in secret, and skillfully wrought in the lowest parts of the earth. Your eyes saw my substance, being yet unformed. And in Your book they all were written, the days fashioned for me, when as yet there were none of them.

Lamentations 3:21-23
> This I recall to my mind, Therefore I have hope. Through the LORD's mercies we are not consumed, Because His compassions fail not. They are new every morning; Great is Your faithfulness.

1 Samuel 1:10
> And she was in bitterness of soul, and prayed to the LORD and wept in anguish.

2 Corinthians 12:9
> And He said to me, "My grace is sufficient for you, for My strength is made perfect in weakness." Therefore most gladly I will rather boast in my infirmities, that the power of Christ may rest upon me.

Matthew 11:28-30
> "Come to Me, all you who labor and are heavy laden, and I will give you rest. Take My yoke upon you and learn from Me, for I am gentle and lowly in heart, and you will find rest for your souls. For My yoke is easy and My burden is light."

2 Timothy 1:7
> For God has not given us a spirit of fear, but of power and of love and of a sound mind.

Philippians 4:6-8
> Be anxious for nothing, but in everything by prayer and supplication, with thanksgiving, let your requests be made known to God; and the peace of God, which surpasses all understanding, will guard your hearts and minds through Christ Jesus. Finally, brethren, whatever things are true, whatever things are noble, whatever things are just, whatever things are pure, whatever things are lovely, whatever things are of good report, if there is any virtue and if there is anything praiseworthy—meditate on these things.

Isaiah 40:31
> But those who wait on the LORD, shall renew their strength. They shall mount up with wings like eagles. They shall run and not be weary. They shall walk and not faint.

Matthew 18:10
> "Take heed that you do not despise one of these little ones, for I say to you that in heaven their angels always see the face of My Father who is in heaven."

Psalm 30:5
> For His anger is but for a moment, His favor is for life. Weeping may endure for a night, but joy comes in the morning.

Ask God to give you clarity of His Word as you begin to read and study each Scripture. Then, give God praise, glory, and honor for touching your heart and renewing your mind.

Chapter Three
Wisdom Supports

"Teach your children to choose the right path, and when they are older, they will remain upon it." (Proverbs 22:6, NLT)

"Family Matters"

Family has always mattered and has been a priority for me. I grew up in a family that knew no limits when it came to helping. We were taught to help each other; never had to beg, only had to ask. This not only pertained to our kinfolk, but also to the family of God. I watched my parents serve God and the saints without reservation or hesitation. If someone within or without the family had a need, then we were going to find a way to meet it.

As I had my own family, that sense of priority and commitment was very much entrenched and ingrained in me. I spent my parenting days trying to find ways to let our kids know that they were special and unique and that they mattered to us. In other words, they were my priority. I never wanted them to feel that everything and everybody else was more important than they were.

We were blessed to have two wonderful daughters. They have been the pride and joy of their father and me. Like any other pastoral family, ours has had its share of challenges. I wish I could report to you that we have always been the perfect family with the most well-behaved children; but in my heart, I know I would be fabricating a story. But I will say that my children were normal kids and, like any other kids, they wanted to do the normal things that kids do. The challenge for them was dealing with the status of their father. Because he is a leading pastor in our city and a leader in our community and movement, I believe the expectation level was set a little higher than normal for them. For the most part, they accepted and understood this and tried their best to stay within parameters that were set for them.

We watched them make it through high school and college and then transition into adulthood. They both understood the challenges of ministry, but still chose to serve along with us in ministry. I guess that helping spirit was transferred to yet another generation.

Both of our daughters have had their share of challenges and struggles. Our oldest daughter decided to navigate the challenges of being a Preacher's Kid (PK) by leaving college and going into the Air Force. Of all the places she could be stationed, she landed in "Sin City" (Las Vegas). Initially I received many calls from her and I spent many nights on my knees praying for the Lord to get her out of jams and to help, settle, and protect her. About her second year there, the Lord in His faithfulness connected her to a Church that was similar to ours in faith, where the pastor and his wife took her under their wings and nurtured her until she was released from the Air Force. She came back home and eventually returned to college. She married a wonderful man, and the Lord has blessed them with a beautiful daughter. Our granddaughter is indeed a special blessing to our family, and we are so grateful that she is a part of our lives. It's heartwarming to see her growing and developing into her own personality. We really can't imagine our lives without her, and we're excited about her future.

Our youngest daughter successfully graduated from high school and college; then at the age of 26, she became pregnant. I believe it devastated her Dad more than me. While I wasn't pleased with her decision, I felt that she made a decision as an adult; and so there would now be adult consequences. Her Dad, on the other hand, was dealing with the fact that she would now have to raise the baby the way he was raised—not having a father in the home. All I can say is that I'm amazed how God can take what we believe to be a mess and cause it to work together for our good and for His glory. The Church rallied around our daughter and us and showed overwhelming love and support.

I was able to encourage my husband with the reminder that in all of his years at the Church, I never heard him once chastise any of our young ladies who had been in the same situation as our daughter. He always said that it wasn't the baby's fault and that there are no illegitimate babies. So, I didn't think he had any reason to feel bad; it was his turn to minister to his own family, just like he ministered to those other families.

Our grandson made his appearance into the world five years ago. He has brought an abundance of joy to our family. He has not only won our hearts, but also the hearts of the saints. Our daughter is a wonderful mother and it's great to watch her care for her son in such a loving way; he knows he's her priority. And, we are proud of the way our daughter has handled her situation. Even though she and her son's father are not together, we are thankful that his dad is very much a part of his life. He spends times with him regularly and they have learned how to be good parents.

As I grow older, I feel blessed to have two wonderful biological daughters, as well as numerous surrogate and spiritual daughters in my life. Psalm 127:3 (NLT) says, "Children are a gift from the Lord; they are a reward from Him." I can't say that everything I did was done correctly 100% of the time—especially in the early years—but I am so thankful for the wisdom and insight God gave me as the parent of children and now as the parent of adults.

My daughters and I have a great relationship. There are moments when they reverse our roles and tell me how I should dress or wear my hair. Sometimes I wonder if I'm the child and they're the parent. Sometimes I have to let them know they are not the boss of me! There is overwhelming joy (and pain) in parenting, but I wouldn't trade anything for it.

As mothers, we sometimes have the tendency to want to be "the fixer" of our kids—especially when they veer off script. Most of the time it's our plans for them versus their plans for themselves. Our next contributors' stories let us know that there is hope when we ultimately allow God's plans to prevail in the lives of our kids. Read on; you'll be blessed and encouraged by their stories.

"God Speaks to Me Plain"
Robin H. Green

This writing has been one of the most difficult projects I've ever had to complete. Offer words of wisdom? Me? Really? And then I thought maybe I could share some lessons learned, things I wish I could do over, or things I wish I had never done or said. So, please accept this as just me sharing a few things among friends. That said, I just want to relay a conversation that the Lord and I had a few years ago. This conversation set me free. I hope it blesses you and has a similar effect upon you.

I remember the day as if it were yesterday. It was so real, so vivid, so earth-shattering. First, I was frightened; then I was a bit angry. Finally, I was comforted and then filled with joy.

"Robin! Robin!" I heard God shout my name: Not loud and thunderous the way He sounds in the movies, but deep and dark, as if He was scolding me. "Robin! Robin! What the heck is wrong with you?" (I forgot to mention, God speaks to me plain). "Robin, get up, dry your eyes, blow your nose, and stop all that noise." I had been crying off and on for months. I just could not stop. I cried late at night, in the bathroom, on the way to work, and in my office. I cried all the time, but always alone.

I could not share with anyone the pain of what was happening within our family at the time. The ministry was going pretty good but I really could not figure out how God could possibly allow our children to get so far from Him (and us) while we were tending to His business. We had done all that we were taught to do. We took our children to Church regularly; we prayed for them and with them. We did not allow them to socialize with worldly people. We dressed them according to Church protocol; we followed the Word of God and the directions of His people. Yet, our children were growing up and forsaking the Lord's teachings. So, I cried out to God. "Father! Father! Why have thou forsaken us?" I cried, and I cried, and I cried, and I CRIED! And His response to me was, "Shut up and get up." "Wow, God, no sympathy from You?" I replied. (Oh, I speak to Him plain as well. I figure that since He knows my heart, there's no need to pretend.)

After much silence, His tone changed; it lost a bit of the edge. "Why do you think your parenting skills should be greater than mine?" God asked. I stopped crying. You know, I had never really thought about the fact that God, in many ways, can be considered the First Parent. I was no longer frightened or angry. I was silent and curious. God is the First Parent. I smiled and responded, "Yeah, parenting. How did that work out for You?" "Well," God said, "stop crying and get up off the floor and I will tell you all about my outstanding parenting skills." Then He proceeded to tell me how He had made Adam and Eve, placed them in the Garden, and had given them all that they needed. Yet, that one restriction was the one thing that consumed their minds and eventually led to their disobedience. "I gave them everything, baby girl. Everything! Yet, they rejected my Word and I had to put them out of the Garden."

I dried my eyes and washed my face. I was no longer frightened or angry; I found God's words comforting. Joy filled my mind, body, and soul when it sunk in that if God has issues with His children, surely, from time to time, we will have issues with ours. Lesson learned and worth sharing: Don't be too hard on yourself and do not let others make you feel bad or embarrassed about anything that happens within your family. If God's children had issues within the Garden, our children will surely have issues being reared in a fallen world.

It was comforting to hear God minister to my soul, reassuring me that free-will is exactly what He gave His creation in the Garden. He gave them everything they needed, including the right to choose. Sometimes our children will choose Him, sometimes they will not. Sometimes their ultimate selection will not come within a person's lifetime.

The last thing God said to me as His Spirit held me tightly and rocked me softly is that when I am with Him in eternity, I will not know pain or sorrow associated with any choices that my children make. I had been filled with pain and anxiety because I did not want to even think about my children not being with me in heaven. So, although I longed for them to choose God, I really won't know if they have chosen Him at the end of my time on earth. And even if I do know, will it matter, or matter as much as I think it will? No pain, no sorrow.

From that point on I learned to release my children to the care of God. We had given them all we could; we had taught them all we knew and loved them unconditionally. Now it was time for me to give them "free-will," along with time and grace for them to choose God. I must treat them the way God has treated me. I must trust that He will call them someday, the same way that He called me.

"A New Perspective"
Marilynn White

So many things have happened in the 4 years since starting our ministry. I thought that I knew everything about being a pastor's wife since I was a Preacher's Kid; boy, was I wrong! I would like to share the story about our 21-year-old daughter who got pregnant by a drug dealer/gang banger.

The first thing I wondered was why would my daughter even date someone like that? A drug dealer and a gang banger with a violent temper, all in one! We had raised her right by God's Word; why would God allow this to happen? How did this dude slip by us? What happened to the discerning spirit? Was she feeling unloved? Were we too strict with her? What happened to her self-esteem? Were we so busy with the Church and our own issues that we didn't see it coming?

As a mother and a pastor's wife, I had so many emotions: guilt, anger, shame, hurt, and more. I felt:

- Guilt for not being aware of what was really going on with my daughter.

- Guilt that I was so busy taking care of the Church members' needs that I failed her.

- Anger because I know that she knew better. After all, we raised her better.

- Anger because she was 21 years old and irresponsible.

- Anger because I now had to put my visions and dreams aside—again—to help raise this child.

- Shame because I was worried about what the Church members would think.

- Shame because of what my father, who is a pastor, would think.

- Shame because the family would always say that we were too strict.

- Hurt because this baby would change my daughter's life.

- Hurt because she would have to deal with the baby's father and she wanted to be with him.

- Hurt because of how my husband felt.

- Hurt because this innocent child has a father who is heavily into the streets.

I had to get myself together because this pregnancy was really getting to me. I decided to start thinking positively about it because there was nothing that I could do about it. The baby was coming. Thinking all those negative things didn't do anything good for me or my daughter. Speaking life into a situation is far better than speaking negativity. My daughter needed me. I had to get past the pain and move forward.

During those nine months of pregnancy, I nurtured my daughter and helped her get over some of the issues she had regarding this upcoming event. I showed her how she should talk to her baby while pregnant, shopped with her for figure-flattering maternity wear, taught her what foods to eat, and so forth. I also helped gather items the baby would need at birth.

When people asked how I was doing, I was able to tell them (without any guilt, anger, shame, or hurt) that, "I feel good about it. This is my first grandchild and I am excited and I am praying for a healthy baby."

My grandson was born on February 8, 2011. This was so special to me because he was born on my mother's birthday and she had passed away the previous year. I was also able to be in the delivery room to see him enter this world. While Satan meant this for bad, God turned it to good! God will take care of everything if you pray without ceasing and believe that God will do what He said He would do.

In the years since his birth, I've watched my daughter become a great mother; and my grandson is healthy and very smart (I know all grandparents say that but he really is). And my daughter does not date the baby's father anymore. PRAISE GOD!

Chapter Four
Wisdom Heals

"But unto you that fear my name shall the Sun of righteousness arise with healing in his wings..." (Malachi 4:2, KJV)

"In Sickness and In Health"

One of the hardest places life can hit you in ministry is through the illness of yourself, or your spouse. In our case, my husband and I have both experienced the devastation of illness and the affect it had on our family and our ministry.

Around our third year in Columbus, my husband had to be hospitalized because of a strep infection that had traveled throughout his body and eventually attacked and weakened his heart. The prognosis did not look good and our future looked even more uncertain and bleak. After all, preaching was my husband's life and livelihood, so when the doctor said that it was likely that he would never be able to preach again, we knew that it was going to take a move of God to turn our situation around. At that time our children were three and seven years of age; we were very young and lived in a parsonage, and we were financially unstable.

I can remember staying at the hospital day and night as we continued to wait on test results and reports. Every report was worse than the one before. I didn't realized how serious his condition was until we were told that my husband would be moved to the cardiac step-down unit because his heart rate was slowing. As a matter of fact, his rate had declined to between 10 to 20 beats per minute and he had to continually receive medication to help elevate his rate. I remember him looking at me with such a look of hopelessness. With all of the courage I could muster, I told him I believed everything was going to be all right and not to worry because he was going to get better.

I left the hospital and headed home to change clothes; and as I was driving, I began to cry out to God. I began to tell Him everything He already knew. I shared my fears as a young wife and mother and I reminded God that I needed Him to give me the strength to be strong for my husband, kids, and the Church. God reminded me He would never leave me or forsake me, even during the present crisis. It was at that moment that I was able to collect myself. The presence of the Holy Spirit brought a sense of peace and calm to my heart and my mind.

I knew prayer was going up all over the country as the word spread of my husband's condition. Early on in ministry I quickly learned what prayer could do, so I prayed and depended on the prayers of the saints. We watched God turn our situation completely around. The heart rate began to elevate and eventually stabilized. Days later the doctor sent my husband home to recuperate. He was told that he could go home but would have to be "real still" for about a month, which meant no revivals, preaching, or teaching. What a tall order! Somehow he managed to follow instructions and the initial report that we received about him never being able to preach again was upgraded to "light preaching" (yeah, right!) and that he would have to pretty much take it easy. Well, that was then, and this is now. I'm pleased to report that from that day until this one, he has not skipped a beat. God not only miraculously healed him, but also brought him back stronger, wiser, and better!

That experience carried me to another level in my faith. So, years later when I was hospitalized on two occasions with a condition that threatened to cause possible strokes, I quickly reflected on God's healing power in the life of my husband. I trusted God to touch my body, and He did! What have I learned through these experiences with sickness? I came through on the other side knowing that God is my help, my hope, and my healer. I grew in my faith by leaps and bounds and I developed a confidence in Jehovah Rapha, the Lord our Healer.

Just as a side note: There have been times that I've had to call on God not only for physical healing, but also for emotional and spiritual healing. There have been places in my pilgrimage where I feared that I was losing it. The truth is, I have at times felt like hurting others so that they could experience the same level of pain I was feeling. During times when my spirit has been wounded, broken, and in need of healing, I'm glad I was able to recognize that God is a total healer. He is not only the healer of our physical needs, but also is a mender of broken hearts and spirits.

It's amazing how your faith soars to new heights once you've experienced God as a healer. Your faith walk is strengthened as you begin to trust God in new and different ways. His Word becomes more precious and you have a burning desire to tell others about His goodness and faithfulness to you. Both of our contributors share their amazing experiences of God's miraculous healing power in their lives. You will be enriched and encouraged as you read their stories.

"The Blessing of Hearing and Believing God Is at Work"
Mary L. Dargan

What keeps you strong in your faith during those times when God seems to be silent? One encouragement is hearing stories about God's work in the lives of His people. When you hear of God's provision in someone else's life, you can feel encouraged, knowing that He will also provide for your needs. When you hear a story of His protection surrounding someone else, then you remember that He will similarly protect you and those you love. Stories of God at work, guiding and directing lives, remind us that God is alive and well, even if you can't really sense His hand on your life at the moment.

Whenever you feel discouraged, Satan will make a move to convince you that God has stopped working and doesn't care about your life. Satan is pretty sneaky that way. Reading stories of God's amazing work or hearing someone's testimony are encouragement you can hold onto to keep trusting and believing with all your heart that God is working on your behalf.

God will never let us down, even when He doesn't give us the desires of our heart. Our heart's desire is not always God's desire. He always knows what is best for us and the best time to bless us. God sees our ending before our beginning.

On September 12, 2009, at 6:45 in the morning, I was half dressed for an appointment. I stopped dressing to dust and polish the dresser in our bedroom as my husband finished shaving. The morning was quiet and my mind was deep in thought. I was scheduled for an angiogram, but hadn't been given the exact date for the procedure. I was not looking forward to the procedure because it's quite unpleasant. Suddenly, my mind was interrupted with words that were forceful in my spirit: "Trust in the one who will not fail you whatsoever the years may bring; Seek to gain the heavenly treasure they will never pass away." I wondered where I had heard those words before. Were they lyrics to a song or a Bible verse? I repeated the words to myself and then realized they were the lyrics to the song, *Hold to God's Unchanging Hand* by Jennie Wilson (Public Domain).

Many times we are busy feeling defeated and disappointed when things don't go our way. We can't see God's blessing because of the fog of disappointment that comes across our path; but we have to remember trouble won't last always and the sun will shine again.

When faced with devastating circumstances, regardless of what they may be, we have to trust that God knows what He's doing. My circumstance involved medical issues requiring many procedures. There were tough times and rough days, and I was unprepared for them. I had armed myself with knowledge about the procedures I faced, but didn't fully understand what would happen after the procedures. There was a lot of pain and a lot of swelling, loss of appetite, thinning hair, and lack of sleep. But, I'm here today to tell you God brought me through! And, He didn't just bring me through; He brought me through with a song and assurance that my healing was on the way:

> He has promised us joy; He has it!
> He has promised us peace; He has it!
> Oh, what a wonderful blessing of healing God has.
> When you cry, He sees you.
> When you pray, He hears you.
> When you lift your hands, He cares.
> Oh, what a blessing of healing He has.
> When you pray, tell others to pray too.
> God answers in His own way; just have patience to wait.
> God has everything we need.
> Oh, what a wonderful blessing of healing God has!
> (Mary L. Dargan, 2010).

I thank God for the peace He gives me. Who can tell of His love, peace, and comfort? I can't express it but I know God is holding me through my storms, and He'll do the same for you. I don't know how He will work things out, but I do know He is able to do whatever pleases Him. My desire and prayer is that He will take care of my needs, and that He will do likewise for you.

"Healing Through Prayer Walking"
Ruby A. Perkins

> "Bless the Lord, O my soul, and all that is within me.
> Bless His holy name . . ."

I give glory and honor to my Savior and my God for healing! Several years ago, I was feeling sick and tired all of the time and had no energy. I couldn't sleep because every time I would dose off, the pain would wake me up. Because of the lack of sleep and rest, I found it difficult to function. I made an appointment with my family doctor, who referred me to a specialist. I was diagnosed with fibromyalgia, a word I could neither spell nor pronounce.

I learned that fibromyalgia causes chronic, widespread muscle pain throughout the body and is believed to be a result of overactive nerves. My doctor prescribed medication, which helped with the pain but made me drowsy. However, I was able to function; and being a First Lady, I needed to be faithful and supportive of my husband and pastor.

> "Bless the Lord, O my soul, and forget not all His benefits . . ."

I went to the Lord in prayer and asked God to help me get off the medication and to remove the pain from my body. God took me to 2 Corinthians 12:9 (KJV): ". . . My grace is sufficient for thee: for my strength is made perfect in weakness," and told me to walk for my healing. That's when I started prayer walking. The pain was unbearable, but Philippians 4:13 kept me going: "I can do all things through Christ which strengthens me."

The pain was worse on Sunday mornings when I needed to be at Church. I could hardly get out of the bed, but I would roll to a sitting position and slowly walk what seemed like a mile to the bathroom to shower. I thank God for my husband, who offered the encouragement I needed to keep going. He didn't say "It's okay, just go back to bed," but what he did say was "I'll see you at Church" after he prayed for me.

> "Bless the Lord, O my soul . . . who healeth all thine diseases. . ."

For ten years, Sunday after Sunday, I'd limp my way to Church with a smile on my face. I sang in the choir and would go from the choir stand to the altar for prayer and back to the choir stand. I knew that all of my help came from the Lord. If anyone asked how I was doing, my response was, "I am blessed and broken to be used by God" (Matthew 14:19).

I don't know why God allowed me to suffer for ten years. I saw my husband lay hands on people and they were healed, but it didn't happen for me. I do know that God was molding and making me after His will and was preparing me for a higher calling. I felt like the woman with the issue of blood in Matthew 9:21, who believed if she could just touch Jesus, she would be made whole.

Then God touched my body and healed me from fibromyalgia! One morning I made my way to the bathroom, leaving my husband in bed. A few moments later, he yelled out my name, "Ruby! God said He has HEALED YOU!" I hadn't even noticed because I had grown accustomed to the pain, but it was true! I was healed!

God had called my husband and me from Hamilton, Ohio, where he had pastored for 24 years, to Detroit, Michigan, to pastor another Church. I had told the Lord I couldn't go because it was too cold and the coldness made the pain worse. God took care of that situation and healed my body, as if to say, "Is there *really* anything too hard for me?" The answer, of course, is no.

> "Bless the Lord, O my soul . . . who crowneth thee with lovingkindness and tender mercies . . ."

I encourage you to submit and be obedient to the will of God. He has a healing in store for you, too ". . .so thy youth is renewed like the eagle's" (Psalm 103:1-5, KJV).

Chapter Five
Wisdom Teaches

"Create in me a clean heart, O God; and renew a right spirit within me."
(Psalm 51:10, KJV)

"Spiritual Check-Up"

Let's face it; there are times in the ministry when you are low on spiritual fuel. Perhaps it's because you're giving, giving, giving and eventually burn out. Or, perhaps you're overwhelmed with the responsibility of home, Church, and work. I wish I could make you believe that during my years of ministry, I've never become "weary in my well doing," but even I have been victim to the "busyness syndrome." Here's my definition of busyness: "Moving about in an insane manner at breakneck speed, multi-tasking, so much so that your productivity level is diminished and you're physically and emotionally spent."

Have you ever been there? If we're not careful, we can get on an express train leading us down a path of futility where we can never get ahead and we're always behind.

Even with all of the responsibilities we have in our roles as wives, mothers, and pastors' spouses, we have to find the time to pull away, turn aside, refuel, and refocus. It's easy to make everything and everybody else a priority and then neglect the One you need the most—the One who gives us strength, the One who provides all of our needs, and the One who gives us peace.

- ✓ When you find yourself becoming listless or lethargic, it's time for a spiritual check-up.

- ✓ When you find that your joy is dissipating and you're feeling dull and indifferent, it's time for a spiritual check-up.

- ✓ When your attitude leaves a lot to be desired and you find that everything and everybody gets on your last nerve, it's time to pull over and get a spiritual overhaul.

There are times when things or people will get on your nerves. So, if you find yourself in a constant state of discontent, discombobulation, and disrepair, and you're constantly irate and irritated, then it's definitely time to go to the only One who can help you get it together.

Several years ago I allowed a situation to rob me of my joy. I have to confess that I was just acting plain old ugly. I had pretty much decided that I was just going to go to Church, give God a little praise so it wouldn't be so obvious that I was in shutdown mode, speak to a few saints, and head out the door. It didn't take long for me to recognize that my behavior was immature and that I really had let the enemy get the best of me. I also came to the realization that God hadn't been anything but good to me and He didn't deserve the treatment I was giving Him. Furthermore, I began to understand that I was in a dry place and that I needed a spiritual check-up.

We'll go to the doctor when we experience pain and discomfort. We'll allow him or her to tell us what's wrong, and what we need to do to remedy the situation. How much more do we need to go to our Heavenly Father when we experience spiritual pain and discomfort? We need to allow Him to tell us what's wrong and what we need to do to get our lives back on the right spiritual track.

When we allow the Word of God to minister to our hearts and minds, we experience the peace of God that passeth all understanding. It's then that we begin to be revived, refreshed, and renewed. There are times when we need a purging and a cleansing, so that we can function with a renewed attitude and spirit. David said in Psalm 51:10-11 (NLT): "Create in me a clean heart, O God. Renew a loyal spirit within me. Do not banish me from your presence, and don't take your Holy Spirit from me." There are many times throughout our journey when we need to pray that prayer.

I can bless God for those times of correction, and I'm thankful that God loves me enough not to leave me in a place of self-destruction. I came to understand that He wants me to be my best for Him.

So, anytime you begin to get low on spiritual fuel, stop in for a spiritual check-up. It will make the difference in your day and in your journey.

Periodically, it pays to take inventory of our spiritual stock. It's during those times that we discover the impediments that continually hold us back or keep us from getting to our next blessed place. These next two sisters lay it straight on the line for you. Keep reading and listen with your heart.

"What's Impeding Your Progress?"
Tatum M. Osbourne

According to the *World English Dictionary,* an impediment is defined as, "A hindrance or obstruction; a physical defect, especially one of speech, such as a stammer."

How often have we allowed the impediments of life—whether physical, spiritual, or emotional—to stop us from reaching our full potential? Probably one too many times to count or even admit! I grew up allowing things in and out of my control to become roadblocks in my life: My feelings of abandonment by a father who was barely there; low self-esteem due to poor self-image; or the idea that I would never be good enough, so why bother trying. We all have had those moments (I see you nodding your head) and the good thing is that we're not alone. The Word of God is full of individuals who were faced with impediments of their own, giving us the hope and assurance that with God's help we, too, can overcome the things that impede us.

Such was the case with Moses in the Book of Exodus. Moses had come face-to-face with the living God, and in that moment, God began to reveal Moses' purpose and destiny. He was to be the deliverer of his people out of Egyptian bondage. But instead of giving God his yes, Moses declared that his impediment—his speech problem—was too big of an obstruction for him to be used. On three different occasions (Exodus 4:10-13, 6:12, and 6:30) Moses said, "I can't do this, I am not a good speaker" (paraphrased). How many times have we given God the "I can't do this" speech, as if God didn't know we had the impediment before He called us? Listen to God's reply to Moses in Exodus 4:11-12 (MSG), "God said, 'And who do you think made the human mouth? And who makes some mute, some deaf, some sighted, some blind? Isn't it I, God? So, get going. I'll be right there with you—with your mouth! I'll be right there to teach you what to say.'"

Here's the good news: God already knows about the impediments in our lives and they have not caught Him by surprise. He called us in spite of our impediments and says, "Just trust me, I will take care of the places in which you are not strong enough or proficient enough, if only you will just obey and do what I tell you to do."

So, get going and let today be the first day that you no longer allow the impediments in your life to impede your progress. Give the issue or issues over to God and do what He tells you to do. So what, you don't have enough money. So what, you don't have the right education. So what, you stammer and can't speak well. So what, you don't come from the right side of the tracks. So what, you tried before and it failed. Try again!

This one thing I know: If I had allowed the impediments of my life to stop me, I wouldn't have been given the opportunity to share with you today. So, let God use the impediments of life to show forth His glory in your life. Our God is bigger and stronger than any impediment you will ever face. Go ahead and take the first step. . . to a new you. . . to a wiser you. . . to a purposeful you! You won't regret it; I didn't! Be unstoppable!

"How Did I End Up Here?"
Precious A. Earley

It's not what you planned, you didn't see it coming, and now you are wondering, "How in the world did I end up 'here?'"

Everybody's "here" is different. For one person, "here" may be joblessness or homelessness. It may be a state of isolation or depression. For another person, it might be singleness, divorce, being overweight, or having a disability. "Here" for some may mean you're in love with someone abusive, incompatible, or not even your spouse. It's not what you planned; you didn't see it coming, but the truth is, you are "here."

So, what happens when things don't work out according to your original Plan A? When Plan A fails, you have no choice but to carry out Plan B, whether or not you even thought about a Plan B. By definition Plan B is "a strategy or plan that is implemented when the original one proves impracticable or unsuccessful." It's the alternative—the just-in-case-this-doesn't-work-out arrangement, or the unplanned path taken as a result of an inability to pursue the original desire or goal. Of course, Plan B is never the preferred choice. In fact, it's often not even a choice but a mandate one must endure, which is why many Plan B's are accompanied by some level of disappointment.

As an emotion, disappointment is birthed out of misplaced or otherwise unmet expectations. Disappointment can be a breeding ground for Satan's tactics in which one may do things, think things, and allow things that one otherwise would not.

I believe it would be easier if Satan just came right out and told a blatant lie, but I've discovered that he most often starts out with a speck of truth that shifts into a sequence of thoughts that can morph into a series of beliefs that end up being far-reaching lies. These beliefs can stimulate sinful actions, kill our bodies, and destroy homes. The aftermath of being lured into this kind of deception can lead to destruction. The Bible says in John 10:10 (KJV), "The thief comes only to steal and kill and destroy. . ." If you find yourself in this predicament, seize the moment to devise a Plan B; or set your Plan A aside for the plans of God who says, "For I know the plans I have for you," declares the Lord, "plans to prosper you and not to harm you, plans to give you hope and a future" (Jeremiah 29:11, KJV). This same God also reminds us that "As the heavens are higher than the earth, so are my ways higher than your ways and my thoughts than your thoughts" (Isaiah 55:9, KJV).

It won't be easy. In fact, finding contentment in your Plan B may take days or even years of deliberate thought renovation and unceasing time with God. By the time you reach the point of asking, "How did I end up here?" you are most likely living in a daily condition or state of affairs that do not offer do-overs. There are some things in life that you can't restart or recreate. For example, you can never regain your virginity and you can never recreate the spouse or child that has died. There are other situations that you might have the opportunity to rebuild or repeat, but they will not be the same as the original. Letting go of Plan A and embracing Plan B and everything that comes with it will require intentional effort.

You must first accept the fact that your life is not yours. You don't own the deed or the title. Contrary to popular belief, we, as believers, can't be anything we want to be or do whatever we feel like doing. We must be who God wants us to be and behave as He instructs. When we accept Jesus as our Savior, we literally invite Him to be our Lord, King, and Ruler, which means, in the grand scheme of things, our life is not about what we want. Sound harsh? Yes; however, the Word of the Lord both cuts and comforts:

> The heart of man plans his way, but the Lord establishes his steps. (Proverbs 16:9, ESV)

> To humans belong the plans of the heart, but from the Lord comes the proper answer of the tongue. (Proverbs 16:1, NIV)

> Many are the plans in a person's heart, but it is the Lord's purpose that prevails. (Proverbs 19:21, NIV)

For some who have been saved a while, these concepts are not new. What may be new is the realization that it really does apply to you.

"It's not fair. My friends and family are living out their original plans. What about the desires of my heart? I didn't ask for this and I didn't do anything to deserve this." Go ahead, vent, and get it out. God can handle it. And, after a temporary time of pouting, you must press on. Surely, you wouldn't make a highway rest stop your home; likewise, you can't permanently pout.

Maybe you did not have a choice in the circumstance that crushed Plan A. You may be a victim of another person's sin and are forced to live with the consequences that comprise Plan B. On the other hand, maybe you had complete control of the chain of events that led to the termination of Plan A, but you never anticipated that the result would lead you where you are now—resentful and disappointed. You may not be able to turn back time, but you can choose how you will move forward. You must guard your heart and mind in Jesus on a daily basis. You must live out Philippians 4:8 (NIV):

> Finally, brothers and sisters, whatever is true, whatever is noble, whatever is right, whatever is pure, whatever is lovely, whatever is admirable—if anything is excellent or praiseworthy—think about such things.

Internalizing this verse is critical because every negative, untrue thought that takes up residency in your mind can multiply and lead to your demise. Counter negative thoughts by counting your blessings; resist mentally cycling through reminders of your circumstance. Choose to worship instead of worrying. James 4:7 (NIV) says, "Submit yourselves, then, to God. Resist the devil, and he will flee from you."

In light of Satan's attacks, it's good to know God does not call us to be defensive Christians alone. As you overcome, you will discover an inherent desire to fight the enemy offensively. Anticipate the time when you carelessly utter praise where a pout used to be. Expect the moment when you find yourself surrounded by reminders of Plan B and you discover how your resilience has overshadowed your regrets. Allow new expectations that are rooted in the truth of who God is to outweigh all unmet expectations.

Finally, it is only when God's desire becomes your desire that you will find true contentment. Pursue His desire. Pray for it to overrule every plan you ever had or will have. Then walk the course that has been laid out for you according to the divine will of God. In doing this, your "here" will always be a haven.

Chapter Six
Wisdom Learns

"A soft answer turns away wrath: but grievous words stir up anger."
(Proverbs 15:1, KJV)

"Managing Conflict"

What's your style of dealing with conflict? Do you shy away from it, tuck your tail and run, or remain silent until it blows over? Or do you face it head on, stare it down, or deal it a blow with fisticuffs? Whatever way you choose to handle conflict says a lot about you and determines how well you're going to make it in ministry. The reality is whether you have a congregation of 75, 750, or 7,500, occasionally, there are going to be tense moments of intense frustration.

I had to learn this lesson early on in ministry. I don't know what made me think that just because I was in ministry, among God's people, that everybody I met in Church was a model saint and had perfected this thing called salvation and sanctification. Clearly I was green, extra green, or many shades of green because I had this weird belief that the saints were not just saved and professing, but they were super saints who had wings growing under their clothes; and they lived in some type of utopia. Silly me!

When I first encountered Church conflict, I knew it wouldn't take much for me to backslide. I thought, what in the world is going on here? Because I was young, I became disoriented, discouraged, and even depressed! I started doubting if ministry was the place I needed to be and at times felt that I wasn't even saved because of my thought life; it wasn't pretty. I had just enough salvation to keep me from saying or doing something that I might regret, but not enough to stop me from thinking about what I wanted to do or say. Well, I can report that since those days, I have grown closer to God and I have matured in my thinking. It's amazing how God can take situations and use them for your good and for His glory. I discovered that life itself can be a series of conflicts; and through conflict, I learned some things about God, others, and myself:

1. I learned that as we go through uncomfortable places, God is using those times to perfect us and to help us develop the spiritual muscles that we're going to need somewhere down the road. While it doesn't feel good at the moment, in the end, we will come out victorious and with a testimony of God's sufficient grace.

2. I learned that God uses those times to show me things about myself. How I respond to conflict says something about where I am in my spiritual walk. Thank God I'm not handling things the way I did back in the early years or I would still be a mess!

3. Finally, through conflict, I learned about and became sensitive to others. Being in the field of counseling, I discovered that most of the time, people who are offensive are normally acting out of their own pain. When you get below the surface and start knowing a person, you begin to understand their pain; and instead of them being an irritant, you can use it as an opportunity to pray for and encourage them. Oh yes, as a Christian, we are required to love our enemies; and it was freeing for me when I found out how to do so from a distance (and for some, a far distance!).

From the early years until now, conflict has been and still remains a part of life and ministry. The difference is that over the years I've learned to manage conflict and, in doing so, I've grown by leaps and bounds. That, my friend, has made all of the difference in my life and ministry.

Shut-mouth grace is a wonderful thing—as a matter of fact, it is a wisdom thing! It's amazing how God will help us if we let Him. Our next contributor allowed God to handle her personal and spiritual conflicts through change; and in doing so, she learned something about herself and God's amazing grace.

"Changed"
Sheryl D. Glover

Luke 1:37 (KJV) says, "With God nothing shall be impossible." I'm a witness to His Word.

When my husband first announced his calling into ministry, I spoke these words, "That's fine. As long as he doesn't become a pastor, I can live with him being just a minister." About three years after I spoke those words, he was called into pastoral ministry and was appointed associate pastor of our home Church. I remember saying to God, "How can you put me in this situation? You know that I have many handicaps. How could I ever be a pastor's wife? The people will be expecting me to do many pastor/associate pastor wifely duties, like speaking engagements. Oh, my!"

Let me be real and tell it like it was. The reason I am saying "like it was" is because I've been delivered from my old way of thinking! My mind was crippled and fearful. God's Word says in 2 Timothy 1:7 (KJV), "For God hath not given us the spirit of fear; but of power, and of love, and of a sound mind." Also, in Isaiah 41:13 (KJV): "For I, the Lord thy God, will hold thy right hand, saying unto thee, Fear not; I will help thee." I had to allow my mind to be delivered from my old way of thinking. I had to ask God to forgive me for being afraid of totally surrendering everything to Him. I had to really let go and trust Him with all of my life. Truly, actions speak louder than words. Praise God! I'm free. I've now surrendered my fear and thought patterns to the Lord; however, I would like to share some of my life experiences. I remember thinking, what now? Do I take on every assignment that is offered to me? I remember an older pastor's wife shared this advice with me: "When you go into a Church business meeting, no matter how hot the meeting gets, do not put your two cents in. God will fight your husband's battles and win. If you try to help out, you will only put more fuel on the fire." This same person also shared this advice with me: "As much as possible, travel with your husband. In other words, don't give the devil space to take over." I thank God for her advice because the Bible says in Proverbs 27:17 (MSG): "You use steel to sharpen steel, and one friend sharpens another."

When we accepted the call to pastor a Church in a different city, I remember no pastor's wife from that city reached out to welcome me. So now I purpose in my heart to be welcoming to any pastor's wife who is new in my city. As part of Berean Fellowship under Bishop Timothy J. Clarke, I was exposed to some good teaching by Lady Clytemnestra Lawson Clarke. Sister C facilitated a pastors' wife group. The care, love, and support that we got out of those gatherings have inspired me to be a mentor for other pastors' wives.

In closing, my advice to pastors' spouses would be to pray and watch. Be a godly woman or man of God. Remember who you're serving and your purpose in life. Even though your spouse is the pastor, you are also called to be a world changer. Matthew 28:19-20 (KJV) says, "Go ye therefore, and teach all nations, baptizing them in the name of the Father, and of the Son, and of the Holy Ghost. Teaching them to observe all things whatsoever I have commanded you: and, lo, I am with you always, even unto the end of the world. Amen."

Chapter Seven
Wisdom Directs

"When my heart is overwhelmed: lead me to the rock that is higher than I."
(Psalm 61:2(b), KJV)

"Where Do I Go? Who Do I Go To?"

For all of the deep folks who may read the title and misinterpret my statement, let me establish that when I ask "Where do I go? Who do I go to?" I'm not excluding or dismissing the fact that we are always to seek God and go to Him first.

Now that we have that understanding, I feel free to say that there are times when ministry can be lonely and isolating. There are times when you wonder does anyone (including your spouse) understand or care. Even when you are sure that you are doing God's will, there are still those moments when you find yourself questioning your decision to be in ministry. It is in those times that you need the support of a loving spouse, a trusted friend, or a supportive family member. If you have individuals in your life who can provide the needed encouragement and inspiration, then you are indeed blessed.

I can remember being in a lonely place when we first arrived in Warren, Ohio. Young, Naïve, and Green were my first, middle, and last names during those Warren years. I didn't know who to trust or who to talk to. While I knew I had the support of my husband, he was for the most part busy ministering to the congregation or out of town in revivals, trying to supplement our income. There began my wilderness journey. There were times when I wanted someone to share with, but I also understood that there were boundaries that needed to be put in place with any relationship that I would develop. After all, you can't bare your soul to everyone, and everyone doesn't need to know your business. So there were times when I felt I was in a dilemma—my needs and wants versus my role and reality.

God finally heard my prayer and sent a true and loyal friend into my life. The house that we lived in had a big kitchen bay window off from the garage, so when someone pulled up, you could clearly see them and make a determination if you wanted to open the door or not (just kidding!). One day one of our members pulled up, jumped out of the car with a bag of donuts, and proceeded to ring my doorbell. While I didn't know her motives, the bag of donuts certainly gave her access into my home! She told me that she really didn't want anything other than to be a friend to me; she felt I needed one. I made a pot of coffee and we sat in the kitchen eating donuts and drinking coffee until times got better. We laughed until Proverbs 17:22 (KJV) became a reality: "A merry heart doeth good like a medicine: but a broken spirit drieth the bones." From that day until the day we moved to Columbus, my friend would come every Saturday with a bag of donuts. There were many days when we sat, talked, and shared. All these years later, she is still a loyal and trusted friend.

I thank God that He not only sent me a friend in Warren, but He also sent me many sister friends over the years to pray for, support, and encourage me. Building a support network can be a critical, crucial, and vital part of surviving in the ministry. I thank God that sprinkled throughout my life are precious women who, in their own ways, have been leaning posts and anchors for me. They have prayed for me, have served with me, and have held me close to their hearts. They have made a difference in my life and I'm the better because they have been a part of my life.

I've heard my husband say that there are friends in your life for seasons and reasons, and I've found that to be true. In the early days of our ministry, my husband and I established a connection with several other young couples that had just started out in ministry as we did. Over the years, our friendships developed into a brotherhood and a sisterhood that have withstood the test of time. We have been there for each other during times of bereavement and times of celebration. The most wonderful thing about our connection is that our children are the best of friends and they love and support one another as well. Our special friendships allow us to honor and celebrate each other without jealousy and competition.

As you look for support and encouragement while in ministry, I caution you to ask God to help you discern who should and shouldn't be in your life. Don't allow your needs to override your good sense.

Where do I go? Who do I go to? First, I go to God because He already knows my need. I can trust Him to send just the right person along at just the right time.

It's a wonderful thing to know that others will be there for us, but there are times when we can't find the help, support, and encouragement we need, or when it seems that we don't have all of the answers. Our contributors offer sound, practical wisdom from the heart and remind us that God always comes through for us; we can be assured that if we acknowledge Him, He will direct us.

"God's Got It"
Deborah McDowell

I have learned that success in ministry (or just success in general) is not based on how many funds you have to get the job done. Success takes funds plus faith plus the favor of God; and let's not forget the fervor (work). Success must be judged according to God's idea of success—not man's—because what man calls success and what our heavenly Father sees as success are often in two different realms.

At the age of 23, I got married and was thrust right into the jaws of pastoral ministry. Even before marriage I was saved, loved the Lord, worked in my local Church, and considered myself a person of faith. My husband was also a believer and had openly accepted the call to ministry while we were dating. While I was not surprised because of his outward drive and love for the Lord and for people, I was shocked and concerned because I had openly said to him that I didn't want to be married to a minister. My number one reason for this was because I had seen first-hand the pull that people have on ministers. My godfather was a pastor with daughters my age, so I often spent time at his home only to realize that a minister for a mate was not to be on my plate! God definitely has a sense of humor, but He also knows what's best for His children. The Lord says, "I will guide you along the best pathway for your life. I will advise you and watch over you" (Psalm 32:8, NLT).

So, God joined me together with a minister; then a year into marriage, my husband was called to pastor. The first year was a blur between marriage, pastorate responsibilities, and a miscarriage; the next few years followed suit—family, new jobs, babies, and Church demands.

Was it rough? Yes! Did I grow? Substantially! Those early years not only drew my husband and me closer together as we walked this maze of life and ministry, but also sealed our faith in and walk with this faithful God. Thirty-two years later I can tell you the safest, most successful place to be is where God has placed you. Yes, the work may be hard and the funds few, but the favor of God is abundant.

Along the way I saw God provide and move in ways long thought to be outdated because we have jobs, connections, and resources. However, when our resources fell short, God's provision never diminished. "My God will meet all your needs. He will meet them in keeping with his wonderful riches that come to you because you belong to Christ Jesus" (Philippians 4:19, NIRV). God's favor can open doors that your money, or lack thereof, can't. "For surely, O Lord, you bless the righteous: you surround them with your favor as a shield" (Psalm 5:12, NIV). There were days when people knocked on our door with arms full of groceries; they couldn't have known our financial challenges but were obedient to God's Spirit leading them to supply our needs. Baby vitamins, fever medicine, and infant formula were sent to us by a sister saint who had been blessed with a job at the number one supplier of baby products at the time. She continued to send products and let us also purchase products at a discount, which her job allowed, until all my children had passed the stage where they needed them. Then God moved her to a different job. God also placed a man we called Dad in our lives. Dad had a job at a baby clothing company; and when our children were young, he kept them supplied with baby clothing from birth to 24 months. Look at God provide! As my children grew, I used my God-given gift of sewing to make clothing for myself and my young girls, using fabrics others may have passed by but, when put together, definitely caught the eye. The phrase "little is much when God is in it" took on true meaning as God taught me how to creatively use what was in my hands.

My kids are all grown up now and finding their own places in ministry. And, although he no longer works at the baby clothing company, Dad still manages to even bless my grandchildren, who have become recipients of children's clothes. We are on the brink of finishing a Church building project and that's another story about the favor and faithfulness of God.

Looking back, I wouldn't trade anything for my experiences with a loving, caring God who sees us and has a purpose for us. Genesis 16:13(a) (NLT) says, "You are the God who sees me." And Jeremiah 29:11 (NIV) reminds us: "For I know the plans I have for you," declares the Lord, "plans to prosper you and not to harm you, plans to give you hope and a future."

The fact remains that no matter how many funds you have or don't have, no matter the struggle or difficulties along the way or in your way, being where God has called you, placed you, destined you to be at any given point in your life or ministry is where you will see Him supply the need. God's got it. We are each called to fulfill a life plan predestined for us alone before time. "For we know that in all things God works for the good of those who love him who have been called according to his purpose. For those God foreknew he also predestined to be conformed to the image of his son . . . And those he predestined he also called" (Romans 8:28-29(a), 30(a), NIV). It is about completing what God predestined you to do, not competing or comparing what may look like success to others. The Church is God's business, people are God's business, and ministry is God's business. Success embodies who He is.

You may never be a success in the eyes of man, who may base it on a temporal scale that changes from year to year or on that which can be seen with the natural eye. But God's requirement for success remains the same, flowing out of our willingness to love God with all our heart, mind, soul, and strength, and our willingness to love people (Matthew 22:37-40). Success is bigger, deeper, wider, and broader than what we can see in the natural. It follows us into the eternal realm. Success knows that God is well-pleased with the way you represent Him, as you are obedient to Him in life and in ministry wherever He has planted you.

"Find Your Place in God"
Doris K. Davis

Praise the Lord! It gives me great joy to share my personal experience as a pastor's wife. While the journey has been rewarding, it was also at times stressful.

As a young pastor's wife, I made sure that my house was in order and that my relationship with my husband was very solid. I knew that I had to have a meaningful relationship with my spouse so that I could feel confident in my own skin before dealing with the people of the Church and before taking on a new role.

God does not want us, as spiritual role models, to reproduce ourselves in others. Instead, He wants us to allow Him to be reproduced in us. I never wanted to lose sight of the person I was within the role of pastor's wife because I realized the job I was called to do was a personal one. I was responsible for my own actions. I found it very difficult to minister when things weren't right in my spirit and in my actions toward my spouse or others. I made sure I never carried problems outside of my house or into the Church, whenever problems may have occurred in the home. Personal problems had to be resolved at home.

As a pastor's wife, you must guard your character. Your character is what you are, while your reputation is what people say you are. It's important to know that you can't always keep people from talking about you because people are people. God may not always prevent people from talking, but He will always prevail on your behalf. That's why a positive reputation is to be valued. But, your personal character, the real you, should be held in the highest esteem. Be who you are! You don't have to allow your title to change you.

You must know that you are God's personalized gift to your husband, and your husband is God's gift to the Church. As a pastor's wife, you'll do well to consider two alternatives in decision making: You can become your husband's greatest blessing, or you may become his worst hindrance. You are a vital part of his life and what God has called him to do. Since your husband is God's gift to the Church for the purpose of equipping them for work in the Kingdom, and you are God's gift to him, shouldn't you be willing to accept the importance of that call? You are his right hand and left hand. Do whatever it takes to make sure the beautiful things said about your husband can also be said about you. It should be and it can be!

I used to feel, think, and say to my husband, "God called you to be pastor, not me." Well, how stupid did I sound? I had to first accept myself and know that God would not put more on me than I could handle. I was afraid of the high expectations that Church folk put on pastors and their families. I just didn't want that. But, I knew deep down within I had to just let go and let God. It took a lot of praying alone and together with my husband. I had to redefine myself. I had to know who I was, whose I was, and why I was placed in that role. My self-concept was strengthened when I allowed God to minister to me on a personal level. Once that was clear to me, I was able to flow with whatever came my way. To this day, I still lean on my favorite Scripture, which brought me through: "I can do all things through Christ who strengthens me" (Philippians 4:13, KJV). If I did not know who I was as a person, God knows I would never have known who I was as a pastor's wife. I remind ministers' wives who want their husbands to become pastors so badly (because it appears to be glamorous) to know that you know that you *know* God called you. You must be very earnest about what you do for Christ if you want it to last.

I learned years ago that it's great to be able to laugh at ourselves because we're not perfect. When you find yourself making mistakes, remember ye who laugh, lasts! I believe God allows that. Hallelujah! That's why I'm still here.

Chapter Eight
Wisdom Leads

"She openeth her mouth with wisdom; and in her tongue is the law of kindness."
(Proverbs 31:26, KJV)

"Women's Ministry: Mind, Body, and Spirit"

If you were limited to only one area where you could be an influence and have an impact, the Women's Ministry is a great place to start. Who better to serve, teach, and lead the women of the Church than the First Lady?

Some view the Women's Ministry as a place to gather for social activities, programs, and the like. While I believe these things have their place and are a vital part of what the ministry is about, I also believe it offers a forum and an opportunity to train, develop, shape, and speak into the lives of women. Here are a few thoughts about the broader scope of Women's Ministry:

1. Ministry has to reach beyond the surface and get to the heart of the issues that women face. Over the years I've come to realize that as women, we have a lot of similarities; but there are also a lot of differences and those differences need to be addressed. There are women we minister to today who are first generation churchgoers. They would be considered "un-churched" because they have no Church pedigree, reference, history, or concept of what it means to "live holy." They face an element of struggle that is unfamiliar to the average sister who was raised in a Church-going family. They're just glad to finally come to a place where their needs and concerns can be addressed. They just want to be taught and to serve. If we're not careful, we'll miss an opportunity to speak into the lives of these precious women, giving them direction and hope. We can also speak life into the dead situations in their lives.

2. Women's Ministry is an opportunity to provide training for women who may not have had the advantage of having a mentor in their lives. At times we can be critical of the flaws we see in our sisters, but maybe they haven't had the benefit of being trained in certain Church etiquette. Maybe they are in need of direction or need to discover their purpose. Titus 2:3-4 talks about the older women training, helping, and teaching the younger women. In a sense, it also means the mature women who have been in the faith awhile are to teach and train the younger women and/or those women who are new to the faith. Training is vital and is the key to a successful Christian walk.

3. Growth and development come as we are given opportunities to function in a leadership capacity. Women's Ministry doesn't mean that you have to do it all by yourself. Yes, you lead, but you also help to develop others by providing opportunities for them to lead and serve. Developing a team of leaders to come alongside of you as part of the ministry will release you to better organize, and release them to carry out the vision. It will help them develop leadership skills that will serve them far beyond the Women's Ministry.

The Women's Ministry can be an exciting part of the life of the Church. Don't get me wrong, I'm not saying don't fellowship or come together on occasions to have fun; but in the process, understand that the greater value comes as you train, develop, shape, and speak into the lives of those whom God has allowed you to lead.

There is an abundance of untapped potential inside each of us. As we stay on the Potter's Wheel and allow God to continually mold, shape, and stretch us, then—and only then—are we ready and able to minister from our passion and beyond our pain with a renewed sense of purpose. Our contributors share how staying in God's process pays off.

"Growing Into a First Lady"
Tina T. Dillard

In November 2010, my husband became a pastor, which immediately made me a pastor's wife. In my eyes, I was not at all prepared; however, God saw things differently. I didn't know the ins and outs of being a First Lady. Being a young wife and mother, I was still learning and growing in areas and didn't really understand how great this responsibility was. I thought to myself, I'm just a stay-at-home mom of four, extremely shy, not the best public speaker, not really a people person, or a social butterfly. How in the world am I going to do this? I was afraid of this new place in my life. I would often watch other pastors' wives to see how they interacted with people and how they carried themselves; some were even preachers and teachers themselves. It was very intimidating to me. But no matter how insecure or unequipped I felt, God would always send me a Word of encouragement telling me that I was well-equipped, that I could do this, and that this was what I was born to do.

Being a pastor's wife is a job in itself. No matter what, I always have to be aware that this is all for the glory of God and that I represent Him and my family at all times. I remember going to a leadership conference and there was a class for pastors' wives. The speaker explained how wives and children sometimes become upset with the Church and with God because of the work that a pastor has to do. Because I had only been a pastor's wife for four months at that time, I didn't understand. The facilitator used Genesis 29 (the story of Leah and Rachel) as examples, with Rachel representing the family (wife and the children) and Leah representing the pastoral calling. Rachel was the one Jacob loved and Leah was the one that was given to him. This was to let us know that while our husbands love their families, they also have to do the work of the Lord. We can't despise the other because both are very important in our husbands' eyes, and we are not to make them feel guilty for doing the work of the Lord. Rachel needs Leah and Leah needs Rachel.

This really opened my eyes to the ministry of being a pastor's wife and the calling on my husband as a pastor. It was my responsibility as a wife to help our children understand their father's role as a pastor in an attempt to keep them from becoming resentful. This would give our family a healthy balance.

I began working with the Women's Ministry immediately after I became the First Lady. Within the first two months, we formed a leadership team and began to strategize. This was a very hard task for me, because I didn't want the women to feel like I was just walking in and changing everything; I didn't want them to think that I assumed my ideas were better because I was the pastor's wife. Again, this was all new to me. I had to move from making decisions for my four children in the comfort of my home, to leading and making decisions about ministry for hundreds of women. I wanted them to receive my vision and me. But once we got things going, we became comfortable with each other. Everything is working out great, by the grace of God.

In conclusion, being a pastor's wife has brought me great joy. It has its ups and downs, but I wouldn't trade it for the world. I'm excited about the years to come and about the ministry that's ahead of us as a family. I thank God for this time in my life because I know He chose me for such a time as this, and I'm forever grateful.

"Don't Miss the Treasure"
Karen R. Spencer

> But we have this treasure in jars of clay, to show that the surpassing power belongs to God and not to us. We are afflicted in every way, but not crushed; perplexed, but not driven to despair; persecuted, but not forsaken; struck down, but not destroyed; always carrying in the body the death of Jesus, so that the life of Jesus may also be manifested in our bodies. (2 Corinthians 4:7-10, ESV)

Beautifully wrapped packages are very appealing. The more attractive the wrapping, the more likely we are to believe that what is contained within is good. Large packages also capture our attention and give us a heightened sense that there is a real treasure inside. Looks can be deceiving! And spiritual matters don't always work that way, because tattered packages can have the most wonderful treasures inside.

For a great portion of the years that I have served in ministry with my husband, I simply didn't get it! I was trying so hard to be the perfect woman of God that I missed what God was really after. What I later realized was that God was after the treasure that He had placed inside of me. He was not trying to kill me. He wasn't mad at me. His purpose was not to embarrass me (or for me to embarrass Him). There was no "super-duper" unique calling on my life. God wanted to burn all of the dross off of me, so that the treasures of His love, mercy, grace, and power could be seen in me. He was looking for His image.

The process of burning the dross off has been painful, ugly, frustrating, lonely, complicated, and public. Nevertheless, God's grace has been and continues to be sufficient. I look at my jar of clay at times and think, can you see your image yet? Or, could we go for making a pet rock and forget the jar of clay and the treasure inside? I need a little humor! I am a work in progress.

Likewise, God has presented packages to me. They have all been gifts, and who doesn't like a nice gift? Yet, those gifts have been packaged in such a way that I almost missed some of the greatest treasures that God had to offer me. Other packages have been delivered to me as well. They were beautifully crafted and seemingly handpicked for me. But, they were not all from God.

Many of the precious gems that I have discovered have been wrapped inside of experiences that make me want to say, "I'll pass." They have turned out to be my greatest blessings. And, the golden gems of truth from God's Word that have appeared to be wrapped in messy relationships or difficult assignments . . . I nearly missed those treasures as well. But now I know not to be fooled by the wrapping. Here are a few of the gifts that I have received with their hidden treasures inside:

- The gift of failure has taught me not to trust in or rely on my own ability, but rather to "trust in the Lord with all of my heart" and not to lean on my "own understanding" (Proverbs 3:5 NKJV).

- The gift of suffering has taught me to persevere with courage and hope. It has produced character in me (Romans 5:3-5).

- And what about the unparalleled duo of grief and loss? They, too, have taught me how to have deep compassion for others who are in need of the same tender care that God has shown to me (2 Corinthians 1:4).

Over the years of serving in ministry, I have had bouts of overwhelming sadness and depression. I focused on seeing the huge lesson that it seemed God was trying to teach me. Here we go again. It's not always that serious. Of course, no banner of revelation went flying across the sky.

On one beautiful spring afternoon during a visit with family at my sister's house, several of our nieces, great-nieces, and great-nephews gathered. Being around them brought much joy. The grown-ups were standing outside talking, as the children were playing in the grass. With simplicity and candor, my great-nephew looked at me and said, "Lay down. Look up!" He was summoning me to lie down in the grass beside him and look up at the sky. Before I could think twice, I was in the grass looking up. Maybe it would be helpful to qualify the experience by saying that I am an early childhood educator. Or, maybe all that is relevant is that out of that experience came a precious treasure that I would have missed if I had second-guessed laying down in the grass at the request of a three-year-old child—another curiously wrapped gift. Out of the gift of tremendous pain came the treasure of seeing the Lord. That day, I got it. I saw God! Through the vastness of the big blue sky, with its puffy white clouds and the splendor of the sun beaming down on me, the Lord allowed me to see HIM ("He Is Manifest"). "The heavens declare the glory of God; the skies proclaim the work of his hands" (Psalm 19:1, NIV). God used a little child directing me to look at the sky to recapture my attention and shift my focus back to Him. Finally, I recognized that God is so much bigger than anything that we will ever face, and that He is always with us in the best and worst of times. I rarely lie down or sit down in the grass, but I still look up; a treasure indeed.

All along the way, amazing treasures have been dispensed to me by the hand and providence of God. The gift of authentic friendship cannot be compared to anything else. Having people in my life who love the Lord and celebrate who He is and what He is doing in both of our lives is beyond delightful. Having people with whom I can be transparent, who can see beyond my marred jar, and who can appreciate the treasure that is hidden inside are gifts. I appreciate those who understand that God doesn't pick perfect people. He chooses available people—broken, battered people with a past, a present, and a glorious future.

The next time you receive a package (no matter what form it comes in), remember that judging the wrapping can be tricky. Don't be fooled. In spite of where you find yourself in this most interesting journey of serving in ministry, your jar is merely the wrapping. Inside your jar of clay is the treasure. God knows precisely how to reveal it.

Every person you encounter in life is a gift. We have been given a great opportunity as God's servants. God sees our treasure, and He allows us the privilege of seeing the same in others, even when the wrapping is frayed or perhaps downright unattractive. Don't miss the treasure!

Chapter Nine
Wisdom Intercedes

"Let us therefore come boldly unto the throne of grace, that we may obtain mercy, and find grace to help in time of need."
(Hebrews 4:16, KJV)

"Prayer Works"

There is one thing that I've found in life to be true without a doubt: Prayer works! Prayer has always been a part of my life. I grew up seeing my mother and father pray. I remember visiting my aunt in South Carolina; and every night she would make us all gather in the living room, kneel down, and pray together. Even as I got older, I would always kneel by the side of my bed and pray every night, no matter how good or bad I was that day. The most honest and sincere prayer I ever prayed was on the day I gave my life to the Lord. If I didn't really grasp the concept of prayer in the earlier days, I certainly did that day. So, prayer has always been a part of my life.

Throughout our ministry, my prayer life and prayer level increased, as I had to call on and depend on God to help, strengthen, heal, and deliver. Prayer for me is a lifeline, and I've watched God move in my life and the lives of others as I committed to staying on my face. I believe in the power and benefits of prayer.

There have been times when my heart has been overwhelmed with cares and heavy with concerns. I knew that the worst thing I could do was worry and the best thing I could do was pray. It's amazing how we'll try everything else and we'll go to everybody else first; and then when all else fails, we take it to God. I know I have been guilty of handling things myself without acknowledging God, making a mess of it, and then sheepishly going back to God, having to ask Him to forgive and help me. Silly me, but what a forgiving and gracious God we serve.

As important as prayer is to me, there have also been times when I've had to call in the prayer warriors. I admit there have been situations in my life where I was spiritually and emotionally bankrupt. It wasn't because I wasn't saved, but I was just spiritually low and needed a spiritual check-up. I couldn't get a prayer through; I couldn't buy a prayer and, if the truth be known, I couldn't even pray! But thank God for intercessors—those who stand in the gap for you while you're going through and working through. I thank God for prayer covering from highly capable prayer warriors. What a joy to be tutored and what lessons I've learned from those prayer mentors. They have taught me how to be there for others in a sensitive and sincere way. That's how you know you're growing when you can put your issues aside to focus, pray, and stand in the gap for others.

It was equally important to me that our children learn the importance and power of prayer. Each day prior to them leaving for school, we would make sure that we prayed with them. Whenever they got into a scrape or a jam, they knew to call us for prayer. It was a proud moment for us when they developed their own devotional and prayer life, and they knew how to go to God for themselves. It was refreshing to hear them say they prayed about something. The biggest reward or payoff will come as they teach their children the value of prayer. We can report our grandson already enjoys prayer and praise.

There have been many situations in my life where prayer has provided the remedy; but just recently, as a family, we experienced a situation that required an intervention from God. There was nothing we could do to prevent or fix the situation. By all indications and by the look of things, all was lost. We resigned ourselves to trust God; and instead of allowing the situation to disappoint and devastate us, we began to pray that God's will be done. I kid you not when I say that within 24 hours, the situation turned completely around! We could not have imagined that the Lord would work out the situation so perfectly. That experience served to strengthen our faith and prayer life, as individuals and as a family.

What I found to be true over the years is that it is vitally important to continually develop, maintain, and keep a connection with my Heavenly Father through a daily time of prayer and devotion. It is through that connection that I find strength, help, hope, and healing:

> What a friend we have in Jesus,
> All our sins and griefs to bear!
> What a privilege to carry,
> Everything to God in prayer!
> (*What a Friend We Have In Jesus,* Joseph M. Scriven, 1855)

Even after we pray, we have to be obedient to what God shows us. Sometimes that means getting up off of our knees and moving forward in faith. Our contributor lets us know that sometimes the answers we get in prayer may not always be what we expect or desire, but there is definitely a reward in obedience. Read on; a blessing awaits you.

"The Joy and Rewards of Obedience"
Mayme Flewellen

In our society, some people think that obedience is only assigned to children. As parents, we desire for our children to do what we say without asking too many questions. After all, the Bible did instruct "Children, obey your parents in the Lord; for this is right" (Ephesians 6:1, KJV).

We know that obedience is far more significant than being assigned to children. God's Word teaches us that obedience is foundational to all of us, if we want to be pleasing to Him. There are many illustrations in the Bible of God being displeased with people and nations because of their disobedience. We could avoid many mistakes in life if we submit ourselves to God and are willing to obey. How do we know if God is instructing us to do something or whether it's our own desires being fulfilled? If we are prayerful and meditate on His Word, I believe that God will show us the direction we should take. This has been my experience throughout the years.

My husband and I had been married five years and were expecting our third child. We were living in our honeymoon house with three rooms and a bath. Fortunately, our living room was large enough to divide into two rooms so that the children could have their own space. But with a third child on the way, we started looking for a home so our family would be comfortable. In our search for a home, we had the courage to look at houses for sale, although we really didn't have the finances to buy a home. My husband had a factory job at Westinghouse Corporation, which was considered an excellent job in the 1960s. We had enough money for rent, food, and other bills, but had not saved a down payment for a house. We had the faith to believe that God would make a way for us to buy a house with a little down payment. We found a home near where we were renting. The home was a duplex with six lovely rooms on each side. It had hardwood floors, a basement, and a large backyard. We told the realtor that we would love to buy the house. He gave us the paperwork and we filled it out. When he realized our financial situation, he immediately told us that he did not feel that we were qualified to buy the house. He said that he would submit our request anyway, but we shouldn't get our hopes up. He stated that if we were approved, it would be a miracle. The miracle did happen because we were able to get a mortgage from the bank. We needed that home because our family was growing.

In the meantime, God had other plans for us. There was a mission's convention meeting in Ohio and my husband's mother asked him to drive her and a few others to the convention. While they were away, the Lord spoke to me and said that Carl would be asked to take on a big assignment and I should be in agreement. I pondered these words in my heart. I thought about getting the family settled in our new home and anticipated the birth of our third child. After a day or so at the convention, my husband called and said, "Honey, we have something big to pray about." I told him that I knew he would be asked to take on an assignment. He was surprised since he hadn't shared the information with anyone, not even his mother. He said that he would give me the details when he returned home. I was looking forward to moving to our new home where our family would have plenty of space. I could just picture that large backyard where our children could run and play; we had plans to purchase an attractive and sturdy swing set for them.

When my husband returned home from the convention, he shared the request for us to serve as missionaries to the Bermuda Islands. Wow! I was warned about an assignment, but I didn't think it would require us to move to a different country! When God informed me about the big assignment, He told me to be in agreement. Yes, we had a lot to consider and pray about. In two years, Carl would be vested with Westinghouse, which meant that his pension would be secured and his benefits guaranteed. We had to process adjusting to a new country with three small children. Of course, our parents would be concerned about us taking their grandchildren so far away. In Bermuda, we would have to live in the mission's building, which was three stories high with just one bathroom on each floor, to be shared with other tenants. The Church sanctuary was located on the first floor. We were concerned about the West Middlesex Campground Missions Board being able to generate sufficient support for our family. Now, we really needed assurance from the Lord that this was His will. We did not share our plans with anyone while we were seeking God for answers.

In the meantime, the Missions Board at West Middlesex published that we had accepted the call to go to Bermuda as missionaries. They had not received a final answer from us. This news had our families very concerned since we hadn't shared the information with them. So, our parents, friends, Church family, and others did not think it was wise to take our young children to a foreign country. We had some explaining to do. The board was apologetic for releasing the information prematurely. We knew that this was our calling. I was still pregnant with our son, who was born on October 8, 1963. The doctor told us to wait at least six months before moving. God sent us encouragement from saints who had stepped out on faith to fulfill assignments given to them by the Lord. As time went by, we received more support. We lived in our new home less than a year and then we moved to Bermuda.

The saints in Bermuda received us with open arms. Our experiences there were awesome! God taught us to trust Him in all circumstances. We had some great times; however, there were times when things were rough. We had packed up our household goods to be shipped to Bermuda, but we didn't think it would be a year before our sponsors could send them to us. In the meantime, we had to make it the best we could. The saints were very supportive. They were our family away from our homeland.

We served in Bermuda for six and a half years. This experience is the highlight of our 55 years of marriage. God taught us the joys and rewards of obedience. That job at Westinghouse that we were so concerned about leaving did not last. After a number of years, the company folded and the workers' pensions were lost. That small house we lived in with two children prepared us for the mission field. We had to live in four rooms on the third floor, sharing a bathroom with three children. After a couple of years, we did move to a larger rented house, which was more comfortable. Later, the Church was able to purchase a parsonage and we stayed there one year before moving back to the states. Some of our family members were able to visit us while we were in Bermuda.

The rewards of this step of faith have paid off tremendously. We are still connected to our Bermuda Church family 43 years later. Our love for them is strong. Our children have benefited from the experience of their parents stepping out by faith. The four of them are people of faith. They love the Lord and have dedicated their families to Him. It is remarkable how God is using them to His glory.

It pays to serve the Lord and to be obedient to Him because He continues to bless us all the time. Let us be tuned in to His will and His Way.

Chapter Ten
Wisdom Speaks

"Therefore a man shall leave his father and his mother and shall become united and cleave to his wife, and they shall become one flesh." (Genesis 2:24, AMP)

"I Do"

There is a lot to be said about women who, through life experiences, possess virtuous qualities and a special confidence that qualifies her to speak from a position of maturity and wisdom. There are some women whose lives serve as models and examples for others to admire and emulate. They are the epitome of humility and graciousness. Well, the contributor for this chapter is no exception. As you read her submission, you will gain insight into her passion and compassion for marriage and ministry. Her story will cause you to think and reflect on the condition of your marriage, while providing godly counsel that will encourage and inspire you.

What happens when marriage and ministry meet and say "I Do?" What does it mean for the relationship? Will marriage have to submit to ministry, and will ministry have to love marriage? Will there be some type of mutual submission? These are all questions that sometimes surface as we feel and fumble our way through the ministry and marriage maze.

I submit that in order to have a dynamic ministry, there must be a strong marriage—a marriage where the two continually strive to become one. Strong marriages just don't happen without intentional nurturing and care, along with proper priorities. There must be foundational pillars in place such as love, integrity, trust, respect, and the like. Your marriage and your ministry can survive anything as long as there are two individuals who are committed to each other and to God. We can be well-assured that God has left a blueprint for marriage in His Word and that as we follow the plan, marriage and ministry can live happily ever after.

"How Strong Is Your Marriage?"
Joyce D. Foggs

The Scripture "Wives, submit yourselves to your own husbands as you do to the Lord" (Ephesians 5:22, NIV) is a biblical mandate.

John Piper writes in his book, *What's the Difference?,* that the biblical reality of a wife's submission would take different forms, depending on the quality of a husband's leadership. It can be seen best if we define submission not in terms of specific behaviors, but as a disposition to yield to the husband's authority and an inclination to his leadership.

Ask yourself if you tend to have an independent spirit or a grateful spirit. Do you work with your husband in every possible way to form a warm and close relationship, or do you demonstrate a current saying: "It's my way or the highway"? In ministry, a husband may be stressed about a Church situation or even become depressed over a family matter. This is your opportunity to be considerate, loving, and understanding. Or, if you have an independent spirit, consideration for your own feelings will come first. If such is the case, then you will miss an important opportunity to commit to practicing true biblical submission.

In *How to Raise Confident Children,* author Richard Strauss cites studies showing that children with behavioral problems often have domineering, high-strung mothers. He advises that if a child knows beyond all doubt that Dad is the head of the household and that Dad's authority backs up what Mom says, he or she will be more likely to obey and will have more love and respect for both parents. My husband and I are the parents of five children—four daughters and one son. We supported each other as they grew up and there was never a doubt that Dad was the head of our home.

Having been both a school teacher and principal, I, too, have often witnessed that a domineering mother would come to school with the strong assertion that her child was not to be held responsible for his or her actions. Trying to reason with that mother often did not bring a positive solution. Poor conduct continued, with the child being sent to my office. Sometimes I had to send the child home to the parents.

On another note, be aware that biblical support and submission does not mean accepting abuse. A woman who lives in an abusive marriage, even if the husband is in ministry, has forgotten or ignored Ephesians 5:25, 28 (NIV):

"Husbands love your wives, just as Christ loved the church and gave himself up for her. . . . .In the same way, husbands ought to love their wives as their own bodies. He who loves his wife loves himself." This leaves no room to tolerate destructive or abusive behavior. Richard Strauss contends that when Dad abdicates his position of authority in the home, Mom usually has to assume a role she was not intended to have.

On Being a Grateful Wife

We can choose each day whether or not to be grateful. Being grateful is a persistent desire to thank God for whatever gifts and talents He has placed in us to build a strong marriage. God will give us the strength to express our gifts and talents in positive ways. "Do everything without complaining or arguing" (Philippians 2:14, NIV).

By adhering to this wise counsel, we bless our husbands and others to the glory of God. Being grateful can also encompass a state of contentment. The Apostle Paul spoke of his own contentment in Philippians 4:11 (NIV: "I have learned to be content whatever the circumstances."

Do you cause your husband to be stressed over always wanting more things: A larger, more expensive home or car, more clothes, or a larger salary increase? I would like to offer this suggestion. Pray about your situation. Don't sit around feeling sorry for yourself. Relinquish to God the things that you really need. Do not try to "keep up" with others. Make the best of your circumstances without complaining about what you don't have. Celebrate what is right in your life. Enjoy the blessings God has bestowed on you.

I'm Blest Indeed by Rosie Stogsdill

I grumbled because my walk was long
And the stones were sharp along the street
"Oh, why must my lot be so hard?"
Then I saw a man who had no feet.

I watched a child at happy play
And thought, "Oh, in his shoes to be
Without a hardship or a care!"
Then he turned with eyes that could not see.

> I met a girl with a smile so bright
> It filled my troubled heart with cheer
> I stopped to chat and asked her name
> And found she could not speak nor hear.
>
> Back home again, I cried in shame
> "Oh, God, forgive my selfishness
> To worry, grumble and complain
> When I have been so richly blest!
>
> With feet to take me where I go,
> With eyes to see the sunsets grand
> With ears to hear the bluebird sing
> And a voice to greet my fellowman.
>
> Oh, God, forgive, and help me see
> With each new day, I'm blest indeed!"

Making a strong marriage requires a persistent, inward desire. "Work willingly at whatever you do, as though you were working for the Lord rather than for people" (Colossians 3:23, NLT). So, let us choose to be grateful for God's goodness and hopeful about our future, knowing that God is with us.

In a strong marriage relationship, expressions of affection can touch your husband's heart: A quick smile, a gentle touch, a look of admiration not only in private but in the presence of others. Regularly reinforce your husband. Don't be shy about it. If you have children, they are watching your relationship. Tell them what a wonderful father they have. Give high praise of him to others. When our children were growing up, I frequently told them about their wonderful father. There are numerous incidents that I could relate to bear this out, but I'll only share two:

- One of our daughters had a serious bout with measles when she was three years old. I was teaching school and my husband realized that I needed some rest to meet the challenges of the next day. He sat with her on his lap all night to comfort and pray for her.

- In those days we held morning and evening services; my husband was usually ready to rest after preaching the two services. On this occasion, I was completing my Master's degree project and he began typing (the days before computers) my papers. He remained up all night to do this for me since he was more proficient in typing than I was.

These are just two of the many expressions of love and care shown in our family. Today, our children love and respect their father. They value his opinions and seek his counsel in many matters to this day.

I was an only child and my husband was the oldest of five children. We did not automatically know how to have a strong marriage. We had to learn how to have one. Stu Weber, author of *Tender Warriors,* observes that God's intention for a man is that he always be an initiator, but never a tyrant; always a provider and protector, but never a brute; always a mentor and model, but never a know it all; always a friend and lover, but never a smotherer. A Christian wife is usually the motivating factor in helping to build a strong marriage. If you show your husband that he pleases you, he will usually please you more. I have tried my best to let my husband know that he pleases me. One might ask the question: Do I give my husband reasons to please me? Some traits will make him want to please you, while others will turn him off. Here are a few traits to consider:

Traits that draw him to you:	Traits that don't:
Giving	Demanding
Trusting	Doubting
Wise	Unwise
Joyful	Quarrelsome and complaining
Patient	Impatient
Flexible	Rigid
Grateful	Ungrateful
Peaceful	Explosive
Loyal	Disloyal
Ability to be intimate	Aloof or disinterested

Our spouses would like to see us as the attractive person they married. Some might argue that it is what is on the inside that matters most. This is true, but looks do count. Sometimes ministers have fallen for another woman because their spouse has become indifferent to her own personal responsibility. One way to keep your husband from being tempted is to keep the fire burning between you.

Linda Weber, author of *Building a Strong Marriage*, has said that when you encourage your man so that he feels your desire for oneness, your marriage will be stronger. There is a description of the personal pleasures of a physical relationship between a man and a woman in the Song of Solomon. We can pay attention to what our men see when they look at us, not just for Sunday at Church, but also at other times. Men are visual and they like to see us as the attractive person they married. As a godly wife, one does well to remember that Paul was talking to wives when he said:

> Therefore, as God's chosen people, holy and dearly loved, clothe yourselves with compassion, kindness, humility, gentleness and patience. Bear with each other and forgive one another if any of you has a grievance against someone. Forgive as the Lord forgave you. And over all these virtues put on love, which binds them all together in perfect unity. (Colossians 3:12-13, NIV)

Throughout the years of his ministry, my husband has had wise ministerial colleagues with whom he has had mutual growth and accountability relationships. When a man is encouraged to be the man God intended for him to be, his confidence soars, the wife's needs are met, and the children's hopes are realized. It is important that the wife encourage relationships and accountability. Don't be jealous of the time spent with ministerial friends.

As you work to guard your marriage, I would recommend that you read *The Snare* by Lois Mowday-Rabey. In it, she helps her readers understand the emotional and sexual entanglements that are subtly but powerfully overtaking many good people. Being aware of the seasons of life can help prevent trouble. The exercise of personal responsibility for one's own actions can strongly encourage specific positive or negative behaviors in your husband.

You will enjoy your marriage more if you learn how to have fun together. Schedule time to go out and have fun, even if your budget is tight. Find enjoyable things to do and record them in photos. Display these photos around the home or in his office. Reminders of your special times together help endear you to one another. Show interest in his world and what he does and enjoys. He can come alive from your praise and acceptance of the things he enjoys. Encourage him to attend ministers' meetings and other getaway opportunities for reflection and recreation with colleagues. Whatever his passions are—hunting, fishing, ball games, etc.—encourage him to enjoy them in the company of other men.

Ways to Fortify Your Husband for a Strong Ministry

1. Be a good friend. A reliable friendship generates warmth and anchors him emotionally.

2. Be a faithful lover. When a man is loved by his wife, he has no need to prove his manhood by engaging in infidelity.

3. Be a woman of excellence. Be like the woman described in Proverbs 31, who is more valuable than diamonds.

4. Be a charming person—one who reads and grows. He will be stimulated and wish to share her with his friends.

Conclusion

"Put your hope in the Lord, for with the Lord is unfailing love and with Him is full redemption" (Psalm 130:7, NIV).

Remember that God has put you two together as a part of His perfect plan. Will there be difficult days, days of disappointment, even illness? Quite likely; but I encourage you to find strength and comfort in the One who loves you more than any other:

> Do you not know? Have you not heard? The Lord is the everlasting God, The Creator of the ends of the earth. He will not grow tired or weary, and his understanding no one can fathom. He gives strength to the weary and increases the power of the weak. Even youths grow tired and weary, and young men stumble and fall; but those who hope in the LORD will renew their strength. They will soar on wings like eagles; they will run and not grow weary, they will walk and not be faint. (Isaiah 40:28-31, NIV)

Remember, wives, submission is a godly mandate. Love and respect your own husband.

Chapter Eleven
Wisdom Loves Beyond Limits

"Will two people walk together unless they have agreed to do so?"
(Amos 3:3, CEB)

"Leading From Behind"

Normally when we think of a pastor's spouse, we do so from a traditional point of view, where there is a wife serving in that role or capacity. But some pastors' spouses are men, who have been blessed and called to serve alongside of their wives. One of our brothers accepted the challenge to weigh in with his thoughts, views, and comments about being a pastor's spouse. He will share his experience from a man's point of view. As you read, I think you will gain a new respect for our brother spouses.

Normally when you hear the phrase "leading from behind," it carries somewhat of a negative connotation; but in this case, it speaks loudly of a role or position of honor and respect. There is something to be said about a man who recognizes the hand of the Lord on his wife and is willing to lead as well as serve her. It speaks of the tremendous strength he has and also serves as a notice that he is not threatened by his wife, but still views her as a partner in ministry. It takes special skills and ability to lead from behind, understanding that you may not always be recognized for your courage and sacrifices. It reflects a love beyond limits that says, "I'm here, I'm available, and you can always count on me." Knowing that her husband is there and can be counted on brings a great measure of security for a wife, assuring her that not only is she being covered by the presence of God, but also a special man used of God to bless the congregation, as well as his wife.

"A Male Perspective"
Matt Flowers

I met Ella Mae Kelley-Flowers in August 1970, and on September 25, 1971, I married the love of my life at the First Church of God in Columbus, Ohio. She accepted her call to the ministry five years after we were married. Ten years later, she was called to pastor the Longtown Church of God in Sarah, Mississippi. I didn't know how long we would be at the Church because a lot of people didn't believe in women pastors; 34 years later, we're still there!

It takes a special person to be a pastor's spouse because whatever they go through, you have to go through as well, as you support them and the family. My biggest challenge as the spouse of a busy pastor was accepting the fact that her time with me was limited, and I had to use the time we were together wisely. I had to understand she had many people who needed her, too. We enjoyed each other and took the fleeting moments we were together as a special time to encourage each other. I did as much inside and outside of the home as I could to help my wife with the balancing act of wife and pastor.

The advantages of being married to a pastor are having a loving and supportive mate who loves God; seeing the love, support, and appreciation the congregation and others have for her as she ministers to them; traveling to various places; and, most of all, being together. The disadvantages are that sometimes she travels without me and I miss her. At times, I feel that I am not noticed or recognized as her mate in the ministry journey. Overall, the advantages definitely outweigh the disadvantages, because the will of God is being accomplished.

I actively serve on the Usher Board, sing in the Men's Chorus, and function as the Sunday school assistant superintendent. I am extremely proud that in October 2012, my faithful mate transitioned to pastor emeritus of the Longtown Church of God after serving 33 years as the senior pastor. We are enjoying this new part of our journey together as one.

I love being a pastor's spouse because it allows me a lot of opportunities to meet many people and to visit different places. A good name is always better to have over anything and will take you far in life. Being known as a man of God, humble, loving, and understanding to my spouse is very important to me.

If you have a spouse who is a pastor, you have to pray, pray, pray. Through trials and tribulations, Ella and I have remained committed to God and to each another. We have stood strong because God is faithful.

Conclusion
Wisdom Honors

"Teach us to make the most of our time, so that we may grow in wisdom."
(Psalm 90:12, NLT)

"Growing, Growing, Grown"

One thing that I constantly pray for is wisdom. I've come to understand that wisdom means far more than simply knowing a lot; it is practical discernment and a basic attitude that affects every aspect of our lives.

As I reflect on times in my life when I lacked wisdom and discretion, I can rejoice in the fact that God's grace and mercy covered me until I grew to a new place of wisdom.

Growing in wisdom is a lifelong task. As long as we live, we will always and forever remain on a wisdom learning curve. One of the ways we gain wisdom is through a constant process of growth. Each experience shared is an indication of our growth and submission to the wisdom process. The testimonies contained herein reveal heartfelt lessons lived and learned. I applaud my sisters (and brother) for their participation and for the courage to share a piece of their inner personal experiences.

I am grateful for the many women who, through their wisdom, mentored, taught, and helped me. They never embarrassed me, but sought to cover me in prayer. They gracefully provided an example of what it means to be a "woman of wisdom."

I am grateful for every bit of wisdom gained through the trials of life, and I am thankful for wisdom that helped me to develop discipline and self-control.

It is my desire to be an example before others who, like me, need the assurance and reassurance of a seasoned voice. My prayer is that I will reflect the many wonderful qualities that were seeded into my life, which I now sow into the lives of others.

I know I join with the other contributors when we say may this project be received as *Welcomed Wisdom,* and may it serve as an inspirational and insightful resource tool for years to come.

Contributors

MARY L. DARGAN is the First Lady of Community Church of God in Newark, New Jersey, where her husband, James, has been the Senior Pastor for 34 years. Lady Dargan has been the recipient of several local and state honors, including the Clergy Partner Award from the Ministers' Wives and Widows Conference in West Middlesex, Pennsylvania. Lady Dargan and her devoted spouse of 54 years have 3 children, 10 grandchildren, and 3 great-grandchildren.

DORIS K. DAVIS and her spouse, Bishop Robert "Bob" Davis, Sr., spent 30 years providing leadership to Long Reach Church of God in Columbia, Maryland. Now retired, Lady Doris serves as an Elder and Chief Mentor at Celebration Church (formerly Long Reach Church of God) where she and Bishop Davis' son, Robert "Robbie" Davis, Jr., is the Senior Pastor. Lady Doris enjoys playing the piano, house painting, decorating, and planning weekend and holiday events.

TINA T. DILLARD is the First Lady of First Church of God Christian Life Center in Evanston, Illinois. She is married to Pastor Monte L. G. Dillard, who serves as the Senior Pastor. Lady Tina and Pastor Dillard are the proud parents of 4 children. In 2011, Lady Tina founded The H.E.R. (Healed, Encouraged, Restored) Women's Ministry. She has found a philanthropic passion ministering to women in shelters and seeing that H.E.R. continually provides resources to those in need.

PRECIOUS A. EARLEY is the First Lady of the Metropolitan Church of God in Detroit, Michigan. She serves as the Director of the Worship Arts Ministry and the Ministry of Communications and Marketing (MOCAM). She married her childhood friend, Kevin Earley, in 2003. As the mother of 3 children under the age of 6, Lady Earley has championed the importance of Christian education for toddlers. Professionally, Lady Earley's expertise is in the field of Marketing and Communications. She enjoys using the knowledge and experience she has gained secularly to advance the Kingdom of God.

MAYME FLEWELLEN is married to Rev. Dr. Carl Flewellen, who pastored Morgan Park Church of God in Chicago, Illinois for over 50 years before retiring. They are the parents of 4 children, who have produced 13 grandchildren and 4 great-grandchildren. Possessing a Masters of Education degree from National Louis University, Lady Flewellen retired from teaching in 2001 after 25 years. She now mentors first year teachers and tutors students in various academic subjects.

MATT FLOWERS is the spouse of Pastor Emeritus Ella Mae Flowers of the Longtown Church of God in Sarah, Mississippi. A retired truck driver from the Memphis (Tennessee) Defense Depot, Brother Matt has spent the last 12 years as a part-time employee of the Memphis City Schools as a kitchen service technician. In 2010 he was voted Man of the Year by Mission Possible Christian Outreach Center, and is the recipient of numerous awards from the local Churches and the community. He and Pastor Emeritus Flowers have 2 children, 1 grandson, and 1 great-grandson.

JOYCE D. FOGGS is married to Rev. Dr. Edward L. Foggs, General Secretary Emeritus, Church of God Ministries. They are the proud parents of 5 children. Lady Foggs holds a Master's degree in Education from Ball State University, which afforded her the opportunity to serve in various positions throughout her illustrious career, including that of Supervisor of Clinical Experience (Student Teachers) at Anderson University, Anderson, Indiana. A gifted vocalist, minister of music, and musical consultant, Lady Foggs has blessed the Church and the community with her extensive involvement in musical projects. She presently sits on the Board of Directors of the Anderson, Indiana Area Children's Choir/Youth Chorale.

ELLA LEJOYCE "JOYCE" SOJOURNER-FOWLER currently resides in Akron, Ohio with her husband of 51 years, Rev. Dr. Ronald J. Fowler. Together, they provided pastoral leadership to their home congregation for 42 years at the Arlington Church of God (Akron, Ohio). Sister Joyce served in a variety of capacities as First Lady of the Arlington Church of God, including founding chair of the Arlington Church of God Medical Board. Before becoming a Registered Nurse, Lady Fowler excelled as a Critical Care/Intensive Care Nurse, having been chosen to serve on the inaugural ICU teams at Henry Ford Hospital in Detroit, Michigan, Community Hospital in Anderson, Indiana, and City Hospital in Akron, Ohio. The Fowlers are blessed with 3 children, 5 grandchildren, and 1 great-grandchild.

SHERYL DIANE GLOVER is the wife of Pastor Joseph W. Glover, Jr. They have 3 children and 7 grandchildren. Part of Lady Glover's purpose in life is to make a difference by serving the community and showing God's love through acts of kindness. Lady Glover was a track star in high school and at the age of 13, she qualified for the Ohio State Track Team. Now she is running for Jesus and honored to be chosen to make a difference in the lives of God's people.

ROBIN (HORSLEY) GREEN has roots in the Baptist Church and Church of God In Christ. She accepted Jesus as Lord and Savior at the age of 13. She earned her Bachelor's degree in Business Administration from Ohio Dominican University and has completed graduate course work at The Ohio State University in the Workforce Development field. Lady Green recently celebrated 30 years of marriage to Phillip A. Green, Senior Pastor of New Horizons Christian Fellowship in Columbus, Ohio. Together, they have 4 children and 1 grandson.

SHIRLEY MCCLURE was born, raised, and educated in Chicago, Illinois. She has been married for over 37 years to Rev. Dr. Robert McClure, Jr., the Senior Pastor of the First Church of God in Gary, Indiana. They have 4 children, 6 grandchildren, and 3 great-grandchildren. She retired as an executive administrator from the Chicago Transit Authority after 29 years of employment. She is currently contracted as an adjunct professor at a local university, specializing in math instruction. Lady McClure is the author of *Sinners Have Souls Too*, written under the pseudonym MaeDeans.

DEBORAH MCDOWELL is the First Lady of the Church of God of East New York, located in Brooklyn, where she has served with her husband, Pastor Clifton McDowell, Sr., for the last 32 years. Her anointed leadership among the women has been filled with creativity, as she declares to sisters their worth as women of faith, with a divine purpose and plan. Lady D has provided leadership to the congregation by leading the Women's Ministry, Life Care small groups, and Children's Ministry; by providing counseling; and by teaching and leading couples to deepen their marital covenants. She and her husband have been happily married for 33 years; they have 4 children and 3 grandchildren.

TATUM M. OSBOURNE is a native of the beautiful island of Barbados, and was raised and educated in Brooklyn, New York. For over 20 years, Pastor Tatum has been actively involved in ministry. She is blessed to impart words of healing to men and women at various Churches, conferences, workshops, and other ministerial outlets for the glory of God. Pastor Tatum serves as the Executive Pastor and First Lady of the Refuge Church of God in Brooklyn. She and her husband, Pastor Kevin Osbourne, are the co-founders of TKO Ministries, Inc.

FELECIA PEARSON SMITH has established herself as a speaker, instructor, scholar, and community servant. Rev. Smith also facilitates women's conferences and preaches on a local and national level. In addition, she has dedicated herself to full-time ministry with her husband, Pastor Michael A. Smith, and serves as the Administrative Director of Community Church of God in Atlanta, Georgia. In 2009, Rev. Smith launched Metamorphosis Ministries, Inc., creating an environment of continuous growth for senior pastors' wives that connects and supports their emotional and spiritual wholeness for purposeful living. Rev. Smith is the author of *My Hair . . . My Marriage*.

RUBY A. PERKINS has been the First Lady of the Southwestern Church of God in Detroit, Michigan, for the past five years. She is the former First Lady at Front Street Church of God where she served with her husband, Pastor Jack Perkins, for 24 years. Lady Perkins loves to cook, read, and travel. She also loves working for the Kingdom and is involved in several areas of ministry, including counseling, intercession, and Women's Ministry. Pastor and Lady Perkins have been married almost 40 years and have 3 children and 6 grandchildren.

DEBORAH M. REEVES has been married to Elder Michael D. Reeves, Sr., for 44 years. She has been First Lady for 37 years at the Corinthian Missionary Baptist Church in Columbus, Ohio. Together, they have 3 children and 7 grandchildren. Lady Deborah is an Associate Minister under the leadership of her husband; lead servant of the Women's Ministry; and Editor-in-Chief of the Church's news publication, *The Corinthian Voice*. Minister Reeves is host for the "Pastor's Wives Forum" on '1580 WVKO the Praise' Community Radio Broadcast Station in Columbus, Ohio.

KAREN R. SPENCER is an educator who serves in ministry with her husband, Rev. Thomas E. Spencer, at the Lincoln Avenue Church of God in Pittsburgh, Pennsylvania. Lady Spencer is a graduate of Anderson University in Anderson, Indiana, and the Early Childhood Education Program at Ohio Dominican University in Columbus, Ohio. She loves the Lord and enjoys writing, singing with the Pittsburgh Gospel Choir, as well as baking and scrapbooking.

MARILYNN WHITE is a Certified Life Coach and is the owner of T.L.C. (Transforming Lives Coaching). She received her Life Coach Certification in 2010 through Express Coaching, which is an ICF (International Coach Federation) approved school. Lady White and her husband, Pastor W.C. White, are the cofounders of Faith Family Fellowship Christian Ministries in Columbus, Ohio. They have 4 children and 4 grandchildren. Lady White is the founder of D.O.D. (Daughters of Destiny), where women are inspired, encouraged, and empowered to receive spiritual and practical knowledge for living and loving the Christian lifestyle. Lady White is also the owner of Gahanna TLC Daycare.

References for Chapter Ten

Heaney, Liz, (Editor). *Promises Promises: Understanding and Encouraging Your Husband.* Sisters, Oregon: Multnomah Books, 1996.

Note: The authors listed below each contributed to *Promises Promises*, and their individual writings are referenced in that volume.

Mowday-Rabey, Lois. The Snare. 1988.
Piper, John. What's the Difference? 1990.
Strauss, Richard L. How to Raise Confident Children. 1972.
Trobisch, Ingrid. The Confident Woman. 1993
Weber, Linda. Building a Strong Marriage. 1994.
Weber, Stu. Tender Warriors. 1993.

Powerful Presence: The Power of Purpose
Book Two of the
Wisdom for Living **I**n **F**aith and **E**mpowerment
(L.I.F.E.) Series

Powerful Presence: The Power of Purpose speaks of God's indwelling presence and inner workings in our lives that, in turn, allow us to live and serve with a purpose. It also makes us aware how important and powerful our presence is to those whom God allows us to touch through our love, prayers, support, and encouragement. It is a compilation of meaningful, daily power points followed up by daily, reflective journaling, which will help us to better understand ourselves, our roles as First Ladies, and our place in the lives of our family, friends, and congregations.

Available fall of 2014

Please visit *www.innerimage-llc.net*
for updates and additional information.

Made in the USA
San Bernardino, CA
26 January 2014